Teaching Children Responsible Behavior

A Complete Toolkit

Sandy Hagenbach

Human Kinetics

Library of Congress Cataloging-in-Publication Data

Hagenbach, Sandy, 1956-
  Teaching children responsible behavior : a complete toolkit / Sandy Hagenbach.
    p. cm.
  Includes bibliographical references.
  ISBN-13: 978-0-7360-8431-4 (soft cover)
  ISBN-10: 0-7360-8431-2 (soft cover)
  1. Preschool children--Psychology. 2. Behavior modification. 3. Early childhood education. 4.
  Classroom management. I. Title.
    HQ774.5.H34 2010
    372.39'3--dc22

                    2010026423

ISBN-10: 0-7360-8431-2 (print)
ISBN-13: 978-0-7360-8431-4 (print)

Acquisitions Editor: Scott Wikgren, **Developmental Editor:** Jacqueline Eaton Blakley, **Assistant Editor:** Anne Rumery, **Copyeditor:** Mary Rivers, **Permission Manager:** Dalene Reeder, **Graphic Designer:** Bob Reuther, **Graphic Artist:** Kathleen Boudreau-Fuoss, **Cover Designer:** Keri Evans, **CD Face Designer:** Susan Rothermel Allen, **Art Manager:** Kelly Hendren, **Associate Art Manager:** Alan L. Wilborn, **Illustrator:** Keri Evans, **Printer:** United Graphics

Printed in the United States of America   10 9 8 7 6 5 4 3 2 1

The paper in this book is certified under a sustainable forestry program.

Human Kinetics

Web site: www.HumanKinetics.com

United States: Human Kinetics
P.O. Box 5076
Champaign, IL 61825-5076
800-747-4457
e-mail: humank@hkusa.com

Canada: Human Kinetics
475 Devonshire Road Unit 100
Windsor, ON N8Y 2L5
800-465-7301 (in Canada only)
e-mail: info@hkcanada.com

Europe: Human Kinetics
107 Bradford Road
Stanningley
Leeds LS28 6AT, United Kingdom
+44 (0) 113 255 5665
e-mail: hk@hkeurope.com

Australia: Human Kinetics
57A Price Avenue
Lower Mitcham, South Australia 5062
08 8372 0999
e-mail: info@hkaustralia.com

New Zealand: Human Kinetics
P.O. Box 80
Torrens Park, South Australia 5062
0800 222 062
e-mail: info@hknewzealand.com

E4881

This book is dedicated to my family

My dad, Wally, the eternal optimist, saw the beginning of the book but not the end.

My mom, Marvel, has supported me and given me my creative gene.

My awesome husband, Mark, whose love and patience made this book possible.

My son Ryan, who has taught me patience and given me the gift of appreciating every child.

My son Benjamin, aka OBI, whom I have watched grow into a Challenger both on and off the court. He is my future professional.

Contents

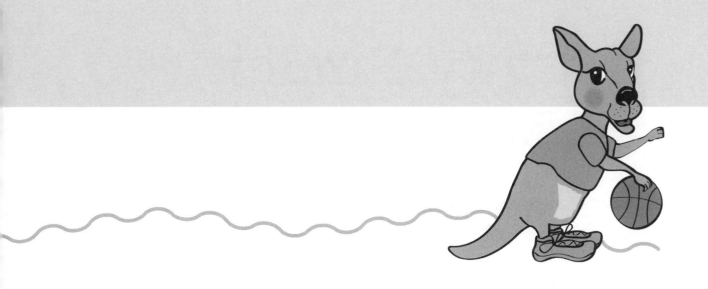

Activity Finder

Preface

The job of teaching children responsible behavior is increasingly falling to schools. It doesn't take new teachers long to confront the sad reality that some children enter school without the most basic self-management abilities, and that this has detrimental effects on class environment and learning. As classroom management challenges and character education initiatives abound, the need to effectively teach children essential standards of positive behavior becomes more pressing at all age levels, throughout the curriculum.

Physical education is the perfect setting for teaching social skills. In these classes, children are often free to interact with classmates and are expected to share, take turns, and honestly follow rules. They are put in situations in which teamwork and problem solving are essential for success. Furthermore, physical education has a national standard that specifically addresses responsible personal and social behavior. There is no better laboratory for teaching these life lessons than the gym. Physical educators have the exciting challenge of leading the way in teaching responsible social behavior to children.

This book is a form of advocacy for the profession I love. If it helps children become successful because of a strong, well-rounded physical education program, I will be happy. The book was written for anyone interested in helping children reach their potential by acquiring socially responsible behavior, but especially for physical education teachers and those aspiring to careers in physical education. My 20 years of experience contributed to the development of this level-based process of teaching socially responsible behavior. One of my goals is to help teachers save some time by providing time- and classroom-tested materials. But I also want to help a lot of children—far more than I can reach in my own classroom—learn to take responsibility for their behavior choices, as well as teach them the social skills needed to achieve their potential.

My Journey

As a seasoned teacher, I have worked in a variety of settings. I've taught in elementary schools with various combinations of grades (schools with fifth and sixth grade only, kindergarten through fifth grade, and kindergarten and first grade). I taught preschool gymnastics and swimming at a YMCA, and presently I am teaching at a kindergarten through fourth-grade school in De Pere, Wisconsin. I learned early that being organized and prepared with engaging lessons that kept students involved helped minimize behavior problems.

When I switched from teaching kindergarten through fifth grades to just kindergartners and first graders, I became more aware of social situations with the younger students that I wanted to eliminate, such as fighting over the color of a ball. Watching two students partner up and not allow another student to join in would break my heart, knowing my son with autism was most likely the one being left out at his school. Safety concerns also arose. I'd see students run to line up, sliding on their knees in order to be first in line, and I'd wait for an injury or accident to occur. Having students follow rules to behave started to seem shallow. Instead, as both a teacher and a parent, I saw the need to teach social skills, skills built on awareness of and empathy for all.

It was during this time that I attended a session led by educator and author Don Hellison on teaching responsible behavior. Hellison's concept of having students take ownership of their behavior, using an intrinsic approach, made a lot of sense, and his book *Teaching Responsibility Through Physical Activity* was soon on my shelf. Becoming acquainted with Hellison's levels was the first of the three pivotal moments that helped me create the method of teaching responsible behavior described in this book and CD package.

My second inspiration was the discovery of literature's power in teaching physical education. While teaching in Mundelein, Illinois, my principal observed me doing a movement lesson to the book *Where the Wild Things Are* by Maurice Sendak. She was amazed to see literature integration in the gym. A short time later I had my review meeting on the lesson. As part of the review process, the principal set a goal for me to incorporate one piece of literature into a lesson once a month. My passion was fired. I loved the opportunity to create engaging lessons that taught skill development, creative movement, or fitness concepts using children's literature as the medium. I longed for children's literature that was written for the gym setting and taught physical education concepts.

The third and most difficult inspiration was my experience with my autistic child. My son Ryan has taught me to be patient, to think on my feet, to differentiate instruction, and to be ready to put out fires and control tantrums. I learned the importance of *social stories* for helping autistic children learn social skills and preparing them for unknown situations. In a social story, the autistic child is the main character in a narrative that shows him or her making positive social decisions and how the situation will look and feel with the positive outcome plainly stated.

Whether the skill was sharing a seat on the bus or staying close to Mom at the mall, social stories helped Ryan. When Ryan was diagnosed with epilepsy, the road became even rougher, and later, the social stories became more important as I wrote one for him in preparation for his brain surgery.

These three experiences have inspired my teaching of responsible behavior, as well as the book and CD you hold in your hands. I have modified Don Hellison's levels to create a structure for teaching responsibility that empowers elementary students to be accountable for their own behavior. My passion for integrating literature into physical education and the power of social stories came together when I wrote the three children's stories that teach social skills in the physical education setting. Hellison's levels and the children's stories form the core of my integrated system for teaching responsible behavior for elementary students.

Help Is Here!

This book and CD offer the tools you need to teach students how to show respect (level 1), challenge themselves (level 2), and be a friend while demonstrating teamwork (level 3). It is full of resources to help you implement the three modified elementary levels.

The book is divided into two parts. Part I sets the stage for implementing this system of teaching responsibility in your class or other environment (such as a youth center). Chapter 1 discusses the reasons for teaching responsible behavior and describes the many benefits for your students, your class, and you. It also addresses some issues you might face with implementation, such as integrating the levels with an existing character education program or with a behavior management model that might be in use in your district. Because a positive environment is absolutely vital to teaching responsibility, chapter 2 describes simple, proven ways to make your class a positive place and suggests ways to infuse social skills instruction into every aspect of teaching, from the language you use to the ways you begin and end class time. Chapter 3 emphasizes the importance of assessment when teaching responsibility. How can you know when your students are making progress? In this chapter, I describe how both formal and informal assessments can be used, not only to gauge your students' improvement and your success as an educator, but as ways of communicating with parents about their children's progress and inviting their cooperation. In addition, the CD accompanying this book has many assessment resources that will help you with this process.

Part II provides the resources you need to incorporate the three levels of responsible behavior into your curriculum. Three units are included, each corresponding to one of the three levels: Teaching Level 1 Respect, Teaching Level 2 Challenge, and Teaching Level 3 Teamwork.

Each unit includes an illustrated children's story written specifically to introduce a particular level to the students. "Who Wears Gym Shoes? A Respectaroo" introduces students to Level 1 Respect. "Where Will You Be After PE?" introduces students to Level 2 Challenge, and "Who Will You Be in PE?" introduces the concept of being a friend as it relates to Level 3 Teamwork. These stories are set in a physical activity setting. They are written specifically for physical education teachers as a tool to reach their varied learners.

In addition to an illustrated story, in each unit you will find games, activities, dances, homework and assessment ideas, and tools for communicating with parents. You will be taken step by step through the introduction of each level, for both primary and intermediate students. An age-appropriate progression may be followed to reinforce the concepts taught by each of the three modified elementary levels.

Each unit includes national physical education standards as well as outcomes and *I can* statements, child-friendly restatements of district benchmarks or goals. My district in De Pere encourages teachers to post their *I can* statements so students know what they are supposed to be learning. This is a great way to communicate to your students what their goal for the lesson is. I present my *I can* statements as a word wall. I put up the term that is the focus of our lesson, such as *overhand throw*, near the door. At the end of class, it becomes part of our closure. Later the word is transferred to the word wall, a prominent place high on the wall first seen as you walk into the gym.

The CD included with this book is full of easy-to-use tools that supplement the class activities and help with the implementation of the three levels. The CD includes the children's stories (in color) in PDF and PowerPoint formats. Posters used to teach and reinforce the levels are also on the CD. Task cards for challenge activities and respect tag are ready to be printed, along with fitness graphs, a fitness goal sheet, and an entire jump rope unit. Communication tools include notes to parents about each of the levels and the children's stories, as well as an elementary progress report to inform both parents and their student of the child's progress toward demonstrating responsible behavior. The CD is a treasure trove of resources; you can choose which materials you want to use.

Your Journey Begins

My goal is that everyone will find something of interest and value in these materials. I hope seasoned teachers will appreciate the assessment ideas and activities that go with each of the levels and welcome the opportunity to integrate literature into the physical education classroom. New teachers or undergraduates preparing for a career in teaching physical education will have a standards-based behavior management system that teaches children social skills and how to take responsibility for their behavior. The wealth of tips and information based on my years of experience teaching this material, as well as the many activities and resources at your disposal, can be useful to any caring adult striving to teach responsible behavior to a group of elementary school-aged children.

Your journey will be different from anyone else's, and this book and CD resource is meant to support your unique needs. One teacher may use only the game activities and one children's story, while another may use all of the book and CD material, perhaps even be inspired to create additional materials to supplement the teaching of responsible behavior. It may take one teacher a month or two to implement the levels and then create the culture to support them. Other teachers may leave this book on the shelf, think for a while about how this will work for them, and then take the plunge months later. I encourage you to use the resources that are best for you and your teaching style and situation. My hope is that I can save you some time and trouble so that your journey will not take you the 10 years that mine did.

I am not an expert. I am a passionate teacher who took an expert's idea and made it fit her teaching environment. My hope is that you, as a passionate teacher, will use my map to guide your journey and find your treasures.

Acknowledgments

This book would not be possible without the values instilled by my parents and the faith they nurtured. I believe we should share our God-given talents. According to Gardner's seven types of intelligence, my talents lie in the kinesthetic and musical intelligences. My weakness is as a linguistic learner. The words of this book came from a higher power, I am sure. Thanks be to God!

My family has given me as much time as I have needed to put toward this book. I appreciate all the love, support, and help given to me by my best friend and husband, Mark. Ryan, my special son, has not only taught me patience and perseverance but joyful acceptance of every child no matter what his abilities are. He was the reason I wrote the children's books. I saw how much he learned through stories, and I wanted to use literature as another teaching tool to help my students learn. Benjamin is my Challenger. I have watched him since kindergarten develop a passion for basketball. He set goals and worked hard on the court through great times and rough ones. I took his work ethic and used it for this book.

Friends to whom you can pour out your heart's fears and dreams are treasures. Judy and Terry have been with me through thick and thin and have kept me going. Thanks for teaching me about being a Friendly.

My school district, the Unified School District of De Pere, has provided me the opportunity to be innovative and to grow as both a teacher and an individual. I have had wonderful support from my past and present principals, Dr. Emmy Mayer and Kathy Van Pay. Shelly Thomas, our curriculum director, has been another valuable resource. The staff at Heritage Elementary School and the De Pere elementary physical education team have supported many of my programs through the years and have continued their support through the learning journey of writing this book.

A warm thank-you goes to the families of Heritage Elementary for making this book possible. Parents, thank you for sharing your children with me; they have taught me so much. Thank you as well for all the support you have given through the years for the various programs I run. And to the Husky students, you are awesome. You make teaching fun, exciting, and rewarding. The levels and books were created for you. Thanks for letting me share them with other teachers.

The Wisconsin Association for Health, Physical Education, Recreation and Dance (WAHPERD) has given me the opportunity to share ideas at numerous conventions and workshops. These experiences gave me the courage to risk submitting my ideas to Human Kinetics. Thanks to WAHPERD for letting me challenge myself.

The three children's stories evolved over time, and I so appreciate the support and input from the youth director at a local youth agency, Ryan Zietlow, of the Greater Green Bay YMCA, and from my friend Sharon Paprocki.

Without the people at Human Kinetics (Scott Wikgren for his belief in this project and Jackie Blakley for developmental guidance), this book would still be just a dream.

How to Use This Book and CD

his book and CD package is full of resources from which you may choose to suit your teaching style and situation. For example, I see my students for 30 minutes three times a week; some physical education specialists see their students for 40 minutes twice a week, and others may see their students just once a week for 30 to 40 minutes. Time is just one of the factors that will affect how you use this book's resources. This guide is meant to be a flexible one.

This section offers an overview of the book and CD resources as well as some guidance on how they can be used. More detailed descriptions of many of these resources are found in the three units that correspond with the levels: Teaching Level 1 Respect, Teaching Level 2 Challenge, and Teaching Level 3 Teamwork. Each unit includes a children's story on the unit's theme, as well as activities to help the teacher introduce and reinforce the theme. The CD includes worksheets, parent notes, posters for teaching concepts and for reinforcement, graphing ideas for reflection, and some resources for specific activities. Use what works for you. We've included a variety of resources so you have options.

Children's Stories

Each unit features an illustrated children's story that is essential to introducing and reinforcing the unit's concept. The children's stories are available on the CD, and they may also be found in the book at the end of each respective unit. Each story was written to help teach one of the three modified elementary levels, respect, challenge, and teamwork. All the stories help children see that their choices make a difference, to both themselves and others.

As with all of the book's resources, you may use the stories in whatever way is best for your class. You can read these stories directly from this book or print them out from the CD. A bulletin board can also be created by using individual pages of the books.

Stress the positive in all the stories. If you question a child about his choices, use a positive question. "Are you choosing to be a Challenger?" is more positive than "Are you being a Waster or a Challenger?" Keep them thinking and let them know their choices have consequences, hopefully positive ones. (Creating a positive environment is discussed fully in chapter 2.)

Illustrated children's stories help students learn essential concepts.

Activities

Three units in part II offer a general guide to teaching the three levels, complete with activities, tips, assessments, and CD resources that supplement the material. Each unit gives a brief overview of the level being taught and then discusses the children's story used to assist in teaching the level. This is followed by guidance on introducing and then reinforcing the level's concepts to various elementary age groups through the use of inclusive games and activities. Next, reflective activities and tools are discussed, such as homework and assessments, along with ways to get parents involved. Each unit closes with a list of National Association of Sports and Physical Education (NASPE) standards and performance outcomes that are addressed by the material in the unit. Throughout each unit, CD resources are highlighted when they are available to supplement an activity or concept.

The units offer a general approach, but it's important to understand that teaching the levels is an integrated effort. The goal is for the levels to become not just a theme you cover every now and again but a part of your classroom culture, a part of everything you teach, so that whether you are doing station activities or teaching a soccer unit, you are still constantly emphasizing respect, challenge, and teamwork. Thus, the way you incorporate the levels will be dictated by your unique situation; this book and CD will accommodate this need for individuality.

A sample block plan for each grade level is shown on pages xxi to xxviii to demonstrate one way the resources might be used in a typical physical education class. This block plan is a plan, not a contract! It is only one way to illustrate how this can work. Change it as needed to fit your teaching situation, your goals, and the needs of your students.

CD Resources

The CD offers tools to supplement the teaching of the levels. Some of the types of resources you will find are discussed here.

Readers

The CD includes three readers (one for each unit) to use with third and fourth graders. Each reader has an article and some follow-up questions. These readers could be used in the gym in varying ways. You might print enough readers for your students and laminate them. Take a few minutes to popcorn read, having students take turns reading a paragraph of one of the stories, and follow with a short discussion. This could be done in one class as an introduction or review of the level or over a few classes during the year to reinforce the concepts being taught. Or you could copy enough readers for each student to read a portion in class and challenge the students to finish the reader at home. If you have a good rapport with the classroom teacher, she could use the reader as a review in the classroom to reinforce physical education concepts.

Parent Notes

Each unit's Communication folder includes a letter to parents explaining the children's story being taught in that unit and the importance of teaching its corresponding concepts in physical education. Included with each note is a pledge sheet that students can sign. (This is a form of goal setting that should be explained to the students.) Pledge sheets can be printed on the back of the parent note and sent home or used separately in class. The notes and pledges are geared toward parents of primary students and are a great way to advocate for your physical education program.

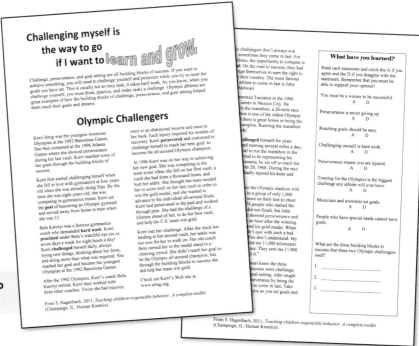

Readers include short essays and follow-up questions.

The All Levels folder on the CD includes a note you can send home with parents to explain the three-level approach. Two progress reports are also found in this folder: One for students who are excelling and one for students who need to evaluate some behavior choices.

Some teachers may choose to use just one or two of the stories and not implement any levels. Another teacher may choose to implement the levels but not read any of the stories. Use what fits your teaching style and the students, school, and resources you have.

Guest Teacher Resources

When you are out of the classroom, you can easily help guest teachers reinforce the levels with the resources on the CD. Kris Boggess, a fellow De Pere physical education teacher, gave me the great idea of leaving a three-ring tabbed binder on the desk in plain sight for the guest teacher. Include the following tabs:

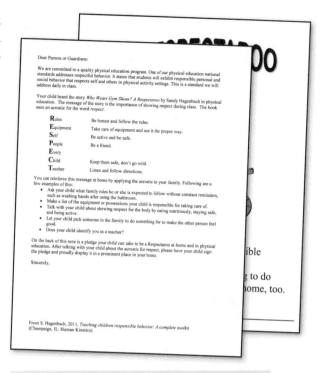

○ School information: Include any pertinent information along with fire and disaster drill procedures. Also include whom to contact in an emergency and how.

Use parent notes and student pledges to get the whole family involved.

○ Class procedures: Include your schedule, a note about the levels, and the note about class procedures found on the CD in the All Levels folder. Include a description of any key phrases that you use in class such as "Freeze" and how students enter and leave the gym.

○ Warm-up ideas: Include instant activities and warm-ups students are familiar with. You could include the Team Warm-Up found in the Level 3 Teamwork folder on the CD.

○ Lesson plan ideas: Include games students have played that a guest teacher can quickly set up and play with students.

○ If you have a strong conviction about your program, make sure you leave a note at the front of the binder. My note says to never play games where students are human targets: No dodgeball!

Homework and Assessments

The CD includes five worksheets for each level (one for each grade, K-4) that can be used to reinforce the concepts for fun, as homework, or even as an assessment. Remember to be flexible and creative as you adapt the resources to suit you and your students. There also are several rubrics that may be used with students. An upper level and lower level How Are You Doing rubric assesses all the levels, and a Challenge Coach rubric is modified for upper and lower level students.

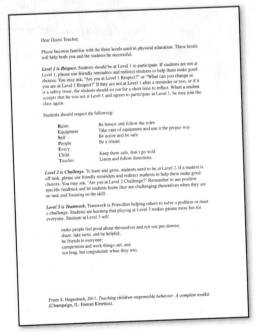

The guest teacher note ensures that anyone can step in and maintain your positive class environment.

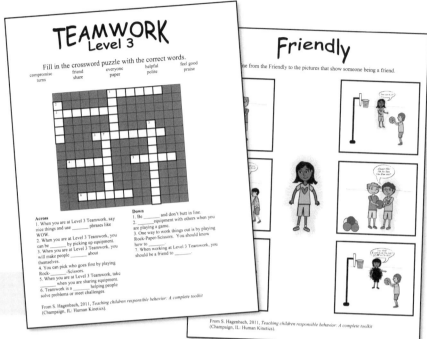

From S. Hagenbach, 2011, *Teaching children responsible behavior: A complete toolkit* (Champaign, IL: Human Kinetics).

From S. Hagenbach, 2011, *Teaching children responsible behavior: A complete toolkit* (Champaign, IL: Human Kinetics).

Worksheets can be used as homework or assessments.

Posters

Two types of posters are included on the CD: Posters that reinforce each unit's themes and posters used in *poster talks* to teach a concept. Any of the pages from the children's stories could be adapted as posters also. More specific directions on how to use the posters are found in each unit.

Reinforcement Posters

I leave these posters up all year to reinforce key concepts.

○ Respect banner: You can create a banner from posters with the letters RESPECT, each letter representing what should be respected (for instance, r = rules). These letters can be found on the CD (Level1Respect/Activities/RespectPuzzleRelay/ RespectPuzzleBanner). These can be run off to make a bulletin board or a banner. I have this banner on the wall outside my gym so students see it every time they walk in. These individual letter posters are also used in a teamwork relay activity and are cut into puzzle pieces.

○ Level touch poster: This is a four- to six-piece banner or poster that displays the three levels and level zero. It can be placed on the wall near the door where students exit. As students leave the gym, they can touch the levels they worked at during class. (Chapter 2 explains this in more detail.) It is in the All Levels folder.

○ Responsibility poster: These two posters can be used to teach what responsibility is. They are in the All Levels folder (the last two pages of the Level Touch Chart). I use it with the touch posters. I put it at the top to remind students it is their responsibility to be at Levels 1, 2, and 3 during class.

○ Teamwork poster: This poster reminds students that teamwork is Friendlies helping others solve problems or meet challenges.

○ Sportsmanship poster: This poster reminds students that sportsmanship is respecting the rules, officials, coaches, fans, and all players, while knowing how to

Reinforcement posters are constant visual reminders of key concepts.

win without bragging and lose without pouting. This poster supports the teamwork reader and can be used with the Create a Game unit you may teach. The Teamwork poster is on the CD in the Create a Game subfolder of Level 3 Teamwork.

Posters for Poster Talks

A poster talk is a way of helping visual learners grasp spoken information. The CD includes posters designed to teach or reinforce a level concept that can be used to supplement discussion of the concepts.

○ Respect: There are 12 miniposters (in the Respect Poster Talk K-1 subfolder of the Level 1 Respect folder): 6 show what respect looks like and 6 show what it does not look like. These are used to review the *acrostic* for younger students. (An acrostic is a set of letters, each of which starts a word or phrase to be remembered. This acrostic appears in the illustrated story used to introduce Level 1 Respect.) These posters are hung by students on two different charts, one representing good choices and the other poor choices. Specific directions are found in the respect unit.

○ Challenge: There are five posters for challenge: One explains what a challenge is, the second describes the characteristics of good and safe challenges, and the third talks of different ways to create challenges. The fourth, A Challenger Will .... poster gives guidelines for effective practice that can be used with any Challenge Coach activity. There is also a poster for primary students: I Spy, I Try. Students search the poster and spy children challenging themselves. These posters are located in the Level 2 Challenge folder, in the Posters subfolder.

○ Teamwork: The levels have been adapted to create a conflict resolution model, found in the Teamwork unit. The Using the Levels to Solve Problems poster may be used when introducing this model. The model shows students how to collaborate and work through the levels. Using this method will help students make connections, practice communication skills, and collaborate to arrive at an acceptable conflict resolution. Scenarios for students to act out are also part of the lesson and included on the CD, in the Level 3 Teamwork folder.

Poster talk posters illustrate concepts to make them easy for students to understand.

Get Started!

Don't be overwhelmed! When I first began teaching the levels, I just had a poster of a shining sun with the three levels posted on it. In front of the sun, representing Level 0, was a cloud, to show that we wanted to keep the gym full of sunshine so it would be a warm and friendly place to learn. Teaching the three modified elementary levels evolved for me over time. I developed resources for teaching the levels to better reach the different learning styles and ages of my students. The resources you see here are the result of years of implementation and refinement of the three modified elementary levels.

If you do feel overwhelmed, consider coming up with a two-year plan. Year one might look like this: Kindergarten through second grade students will have the three children's stories read to them to introduce the three levels, along with a few selected activities. Students in third and fourth grade may have a poster talk to introduce the levels, along with a few selected activities. You and your students can work on using the common language and being consistent over the rest of the year. This way you will start building the culture of your gym. In year two, you might add more activities and progressions while continuing to build the positive culture the levels will bring to your gym. Alternatively, you might choose to just read the children's stories the first year you implement the levels and add the poster talks the following year.

Let your journey of implementing the levels evolve at a speed that is right for you. Use these resources to fit the needs of your students, your school, and you. Adapt as needed. Remember to always be positive and consistent in your expectations. Have fun and be creative with whatever resources you use to teach or reinforce the concepts of respect, responsibility, challenge, sportsmanship, and teamwork. Do what is right for you, but do make the leap. You won't regret it!

KINDERGARTEN BLOCK PLAN

Time, level, and emphasis	Activities
Day 1 Respect	Read Respectaroo story Practice Freeze and Go Incorporate Level Touch Poster
Day 2 Respect	Poster talk Practice finding safe space and review boundaries Review Level Touch Poster or Respect Graph Hand out Parent Note and Pledge
Day 3 Respect: Make connections	Name games: start learning names Review Level Touch Poster or Respect Graph
Day 4 Respect: Teamwork	Introduce parachute play Teamwork is Friendlies helping others meet challenges or solve problems. Your teacher is the coach. Use level 1 respect to follow the coach's instructions so the team can meet the challenges. Review Level Touch Poster or Respect Graph
When students know safe space and boundaries and can follow simple directions, begin Challenge	Explain what a challenge is: think, practice, and make skill harder if it is too easy I Spy, I Try poster Play Splash (p. 81) Review Level Touch Poster or Challenge Graph
When students know safe space and boundaries and can follow simple directions, reinforce Respect	Play Pigs Out of the Pen (p. 39) Focus on being honest with rules Focus on sharing balls Review Level Touch Poster or Respect Graph
(4-6 weeks into school) Day 1 Teamwork	Common Mixer warm-up (p. 122) Read Friendlies story Play Puppies and Penguins (Rock-Paper-Scissors) (p. 124) Do Share and Catch Relay (p.126) Review Teamwork Graph
Day 2 Teamwork	Warm up with Common Mixer (p. 122) Sit down with partner by marker board Create class praise phrase Review Rock-Paper-Scissors Begin Taking-Turns Stations (p. 125)—use praise phrase Review Teamwork Graph
Day 3 Teamwork	Warm up Divide class in half Play Team Scoop (p. 127) Do Partner Dance (p. 123) Review Teamwork Graph
Day 4 Teamwork	Warm up with Common Mixer (p. 122) Review Rock-Paper-Scissors Assign Good Sports Around the Town (p. 127) Review Teamwork Graph

(continued)

KINDERGARTEN BLOCK PLAN *(continued)*

Time, level, and emphasis	Activities
Winter activity: Teamwork	Warm up with Winter Wonderland (p. 130) Play Jack Frost Tag (p. 131) Review Level Touch Poster
Every class, every level	Use teachable moments to reinforce levels
Reflection (when appropriate)	Review Level Touch Poster Use reflective graphs Draw a picture Explain How Are You Doing Assessment

FIRST GRADE BLOCK PLAN

Time, level, and emphasis	Activities
Day 1 Respect	Read Respectaroo story Practice Freeze and Go Do Freeze Dance (p. 34) Review Level Touch Poster
Day 2 Respect	Put in squads or in special spots to start class Conduct Poster Talk Play Pigs Out of the Pen (p. 39) Review Level Touch Poster or Respect Graph Hand out Parent Note and Pledge
Day 3 Respect: Make connections	Name games; start learning names Review Level Touch Poster or Respect Graph
Day 4 Challenge	Begin with instant activity Explain what a challenge is: Think, practice, make skill harder if it is too easy; or, read Challenger story and hand out Parent Note and Pledge Play Spiders in the Web (p. 81) Review Level Touch Poster or Challenge Graph
Day 5 Teamwork	Engage in parachute play Teamwork is Friendlies helping others meet challenges or solve problems. Your teacher is the coach. Use level 1 respect to follow the coach's instructions so the team can meet the challenges. Review Level Touch Poster or Respect Graph
(4-6 weeks into school) Day 1 Teamwork	Warm up with Common Mixer (p. 122) Read Friendlies story Play Puppies and Penguins (Rock-Paper-Scissors) (p. 124) Do Share and Catch Relay (p. 126) Review Teamwork Graph
Day 2 Teamwork	Warm up with Common Mixer (p. 122) Sit down with partner by marker board Create class praise phrase Review Rock-Paper-Scissors Assign Taking-Turns Stations (p. 125); use praise phrase Review Teamwork Graph
Day 3 Teamwork	Warm up Divide class in half Play Team Scoop (p. 127) Do Partner Dance (p. 123) Review Teamwork Graph
Day 4 Teamwork	Warm up with Common Mixer (p. 122) Review Rock-Paper-Scissors Assign Good Sports Around the Town (p. 127) Review Teamwork Graph

(continued)

FIRST GRADE BLOCK PLAN *(continued)*

Time, level, and emphasis	Activities
(Later in the year) Challenge	Jump Rope Skill Challenge: Introduce Big 10 Club Modified Challenge Coach activity (p. 91) Challenge graph Modified Challenge Coach assessment
(Winter activity) Teamwork	Warm up with Winter Wonderland (p. 130) Play Jack Frost Tag (p. 131) Review Level Touch Poster
(Later in the year) Teamwork Respect	Teams Add Up (p. 122) Play Ocean Kingdom (p. 131) Review Level Touch Poster Scooter City (p. 42)
Every class, every level	Use teachable moments to reinforce levels
Reflection (when appropriate)	Review Level Touch Poster or reflective graph Draw a line to or circle picture Do How Are You Doing Assessment

SECOND GRADE BLOCK PLAN

Time, level, and emphasis	Activities
Day 1 Respect	Conduct Poster Talk: Review what previous classes wrote on the chart. Ask the class if there is anything they would like to add. Do Respect Dance (p. 35) Play Respect Tag (p. 36)
Day 2 Respect	Conduct instant activity Put in squads or on special spots to start class Play Pigs Out of the Pen (p. 39)
Day 3 Respect: Make connections	Play name games: start learning names (If you have had these students for the last two years and know them well, then you may want to skip this lesson if time is tight.)
Day 4 Challenge	Conduct instant activity Read Challenger story Conduct Challenge Poster Talk and play Spiders in the Web (p. 81) or do Challenge Poster Talk and Challenge Graph
Optional challenge day	Conduct instant activity Review what a challenge is Do Challenge Stations (p. 82) or Challenge Graph
Day 5 Teamwork	Engage in parachute play or other cooperative activity
(Second or third week) Day 1 Challenge Goal Day	Make an overhead of Goal Sheet Have one Goal Sheet for each student Explain how to get a score and exactly where to write the score Assign students to goal stations Review Level Touch Poster or Challenge Graph
Day 2 Challenge Goal Day	Finish taking scores Review Level Touch Poster or Challenge Graph
Day 3 Challenge Goal Day	Make goals If time allows, start checking to see if students can reach their goals, then have students try to reach goals monthly Review Level Touch Poster or Challenge Graph
(Once a month throughout year) Challenge Goal Day	Try to reach goals Review Level Touch Poster or Challenge Graph
(Later in the year) Challenge	Jump Rope Skill Challenge: Introduce Alphabet Club Modified Challenge Coach activity (p. 91) Challenge Graph Modified Challenge Coach assessment

(continued)

SECOND GRADE BLOCK PLAN   *(continued)*

Time, level, and emphasis	Activities
(4-6 weeks into school) Day 1 Teamwork	Warm up with Common Mixer (p. 122) Read Friendlies story Play Puppies and Penguins (Rock-Paper-Scissors) (p. 124) Do Share and Catch Relay (p. 126) Review Teamwork Graph
Day 2 Teamwork	Warm up with Common Mixer (p. 122) Sit down with partner by marker board Create class praise phrase Review Rock-Paper-Scissors Do Taking-Turns Stations (p. 125)—use praise phrase Review Teamwork Graph
Day 3 Teamwork	Warm up Divide class in half Play Team Scoop (p. 127) Do Partner Dance (p. 123) Review Teamwork Graph
Day 4 Teamwork	Warm up with Common Mixer (p. 122) Review Rock-Paper-Scissors Assign Good Sports Around the Town (p. 127) Review Teamwork Graph
(Midyear) Teamwork conflict resolution	Introduce process with poster talk Have 4-5 groups each solve a scenario
(Any time) Teamwork	Teams Add Up (p. 122) Play Ocean Kingdom (p. 131) Review Level Touch Poster
(Later in the year) Respect	Scooter City (p. 42) Review Level Touch Poster
Every class, every level	Use teachable moments to reinforce levels
Reflection (when appropriate)	Review Level Touch Poster or reflective graph Assign word searches Use How Are You Doing Assessment or Challenge Assessment

THIRD GRADE BLOCK PLAN

Time, level, and emphasis	Activities
Day 1 Respect	Conduct Poster Talk: Review what previous classes wrote on the chart; ask the class if there is anything they would like to add Do Respect Dance (p. 35) Play Respect Tag (p. 36)
Day 2 Respect	Conduct instant activity Put in squads or on special spots to start class (do Respect Chant with squat thrusts or jumping jacks) Play Pigs Out of the Pen (p. 39) Review Level Touch Poster
Day 3 Respect: Make connections	Play name games: Start learning names (If you have had these students for the last three years and know them well, then you may want to skip this lesson if time is tight.)
Day 4 Challenge	Conduct instant activity Consider reading Challenger story, concentrating on how the challenges were made Conduct Challenge Poster Talk: Definition of a Challenge, Characteristics of a Challenge, and Creating Challenges Do Challenge Stations (p. 82) Reflect on how students made challenges Review Level Touch Poster or Challenge Graph
Day 5 Teamwork	Conduct team warm-up using the team warm-up cards Reflect and list what good characteristics of teamwork they saw in the warm-up and what could be improved. Create a Definition (p. 132) Post definitions in gym Play a tag game where students must use teamwork to save frozen people
Day 6 Teamwork	Start a cooperative unit or Create a Game unit (p. 134)
Teamwork conflict resolution (when needed)	Review process with poster talk Have class resolve one scenario or have 4-5 groups each solve a scenario
(Any time) Teamwork	Teams Add Up (p. 122) Play Ocean Kingdom (p. 131) Review Level Touch Poster
(Later in the year) Challenge	Jump Rope Skill Challenge: Review Jump Rope Skill Sheet Challenge Coach activity (p. 91) Challenge graph Challenge Coach assessment
Every class, every level	Use teachable moments to reinforce levels
Reflection (when appropriate)	Review Level Touch Poster or reflective graph Assign crossword puzzles Review How Are You Doing Assessment or Challenge Assessment

FOURTH GRADE BLOCK PLAN

Time, level, and emphasis	Activities
Day 1 Respect	Put class in squads Review respect using Respect Banner Explain Respect Puzzle Relay and Every Child questionnaire (p. 41) Students do questionnaire and then play Respect Puzzle Relay If there is extra time, do Respect Dance (p. 35) or play Respect Tag (p. 36)
Day 2 Respect: Make connections	Play name games: start learning names (If you have had these students for the last four years and know them well, then you may want to skip this lesson if time is tight.)
Day 3 Challenge	Conduct instant activity Conduct Challenge Poster Talk: Definition of a Challenge, Characteristics of a Challenge, and Creating Challenges Do Challenge Stations (p. 82) Reflect on how students made challenges
Day 4 Teamwork	Conduct team warm-up using the team warm-up cards Reflect and list what good characteristics of teamwork were obesrved in the warm-up and what could be improved Create a Definition (p. 132) From two lists, create a class definition of teamwork Post definitions in gym, hall, or classroom Play a tag game where students must use teamwork to save frozen people
Day 5 Teamwork	Start a teambuilding unit
Teamwork conflict resolution (when needed)	Review process with Poster Talk Have class resolve one conflict scenario or have 4-5 groups each solve a scenario
Challenge: Goal-setting fitness unit	Make an overhead of a Fitness Graph and the Fitness Goal Sheet Hand out fitness scores Have students graph their fitness scores Using information from fitness graphs, students write a fitness goal
(Any time) Teamwork	Teams Add Up (p. 122) Play Ocean Kingdom (p. 131) Review Level Touch Poster
(Later in the year) Challenge	Jump Rope Skill Challenge: Review Jump Rope Skill Sheet Challenge Coach activity (p. 91) Challenge graph Challenge Coach assessment
Every class, every level	Use teachable moments to reinforce levels
Reflection (when appropriate)	Review Level Touch Poster or reflective graph Apply it outside of PE Read from readers Complete How Are You Doing Assessment

PART I

Preparing to Teach Responsible Behavior

chapter 1

Why Teach Responsible Behavior?

Why is teaching responsible behavior so important? Is it because national standards tell us it is? Is it because responsible students can make our lives easier as teachers or group leaders? Or is it because it is right for kids? We may answer yes to all of these reasons, but most of all, it's to help children be the best they can be. The only way for them to reach their true potential is through responsible behavior: showing respect, challenging themselves, and working well with others in a team environment. These are all skills they will need to be productive citizens in the 21st century.

What Is Responsible Behavior?

In 1994, I was teaching kindergarten and first grade part-time and managing student behavior with an assertive discipline model that included charts and rewards. It took a lot of time at the end of class to mark the chart and discuss the five or so rules that I had. The students were fairly well behaved, but I spent too much time talking about their behavior during class and at the end of class.

I became increasingly frustrated with some of the behaviors I observed. Why wouldn't students share? I'd see arguments over whatever piece of equipment was perceived as the prize—for example, some students just *had* to have the blue ball, and a tug of war would break out. Why couldn't they play ball together? Why couldn't they just be happy they had equipment to play with?

Students love to be first, whether it is being the first to take a turn or the first in line to go back to class. What's the big deal? Everyone will get a turn. Everyone will get back to the classroom at about the same time. The arguing, the running, and the pushing over the line order were wearing on my nerves.

During an individualized education program (IEP) discussion about my son Ryan, I expressed concern over his lack of friends. I was told by his second-grade special education teacher that he may never have friends. At the time he was not yet diagnosed with autism, and the comment came as a shock. She was right. Perhaps because of Ryan, perhaps because of a soft spot in my heart, any time I saw a student left out or rejected it would hurt. Why did they argue over who got to play with whom? Why couldn't students be happy playing with any one of their classmates? Why were they hurtful with their comments?

Having worked in a school district that didn't have much equipment, I quickly learned to appreciate any equipment I could lay my hands on. Like lots of teachers, sometimes I would pick up little things on sale and pay for them out of my own pocket. Once I bought some cheap foam paddles, and I was very excited to use them with balloons in class the next day. But it wasn't long before the handles were cracking, and the foam had been picked at. Was this because the equipment was inexpensive, or because the students weren't treating it with respect? If the paddle had been theirs, would they have picked at it?

And why must students find new, sometimes dangerous, uses for equipment?. A cone becomes a hat or megaphone instead of a marker. A poly spot becomes a Frisbee and a jump rope a helicopter propeller. We do want creative students, but we also want our equipment used the correct way so everyone is safe, and the equipment lasts.

Most students love to move, but there are always a few trying to find ways to get out of work. Certain students always seem to need to get a drink or use the bathroom during skill practice time. These same students have shoes that just can't stay tied once they start jogging. Then there is the student who, while practicing throwing at a target, begins throwing at the student next to him. Wouldn't it be great if students had an inner drive to do their best?

With these frustrations on my mind, I attended a workshop at the University of Wisconsin at La Crosse that featured a session by educator Don Hellison on teaching responsible behavior. He identified a loose progression of five *awareness levels* or *behavior levels* that teachers and students can consider to be goals (Hellison 2003):

Level Zero, Irresponsibility. Students blame others and make excuses for their behavior choices.

Level I, Respect. Students can control their behavior and don't interfere in other people's right to learn or teach. They may not always participate or show effort.

Level II, Participation. Students show some respect, participate willingly, and practice under teacher's supervision.

Level III, Self-Direction. Students show respect and participate on their own, starting to identify their needs in skill development and then making a plan to meet their needs.

Level IV, Caring. Students show respect, participate with self-direction, and cooperate with others by helping, supporting, and showing concern.

I felt that this type of approach offered a lot of promise, but I wasn't sure how to integrate these levels in my own teaching. The levels were too wordy for primary students, and I struggled with explaining what self-direction was. I was tired of so many wordy rules. I tried to create a one-rule class environment—show respect—but something was still missing. So I tried modifying Hellison's levels for the elementary students I was teaching in the following ways:

o I simplified the language a bit. I chose three words to represent the levels that I thought would be easy for kids this age to remember, and I focused the teaching of those levels on principles kids can understand, like safety and friendship.

o I used Arabic numerals rather than Roman.

o I combined Hellison's levels II and III into one elementary level.

The modifications resulted in the following elementary levels of responsible behavior.

Level 0 Disrespect and Irresponsibility. Students are not at Level 1 Respect. (This level is not an emphasis of the model. The focus is on the three levels of positive behavior.)

Level 1 Respect: Students show RESPECT for all of the following, presented in an acrostic to aid memory:

- **R**ules—Be honest and follow the rules.
- **E**quipment—Take care of equipment and use it the proper way.
- **S**elf—Be active and be safe.
- **P**eople—Be a friend.
- **E**very—No matter how they look, what abilities they have, what they own, how old they are, or if they are boys or girls.
- **C**hild—Keep them safe; don't go wild.
- **T**eacher—Listen and follow directions.

Level 2 Challenge. When learning or practicing skills, students think about form and try to meet the teacher's challenge. If the challenge is too easy or is met, the students then should challenge themselves. The challenge should be safe, not interfere with others, and be met with practice, not luck. (This level combined Hellison's level II participation and III self-direction.)

Level 3 Teamwork. When participating in activities, students help others to solve problems or meet challenges. They aspire to be *Friendlies* who share, take turns, are helpful, compromise, are polite, do not brag but congratulate, are friends to everyone, and make people feel good about themselves.

So when we talk in this book about responsible behavior, for the purposes of our teaching we're thinking of it as helping our students exhibit respect, accept and meet challenges, and work with others in a team environment. The levels that represent these behaviors have become my structure for managing behavior and integrating character education into my physical education classes.

My pet peeves are now teachable moments. I don't stress over these common gym behaviors. I now have the tools, common language, and resources to teach my students what good behavior choices look and feel like through the three modified elementary levels.

Benefits of Teaching Responsible Behavior

Teaching responsible personal and social behavior can make a teacher or leader's job easier, more effective, and more rewarding. There is less stress when students act responsibly and are respectful. Behavior management time is saved, there is more time for teaching, and students spend more time on task. We feel more fulfilled, and we are closer to reaching our potential as effective teachers. Yes, life is easier, but that is because our students are more successful.

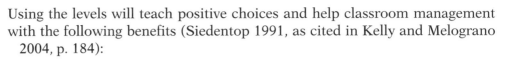

Using the levels will teach positive choices and help classroom management with the following benefits (Siedentop 1991, as cited in Kelly and Melograno 2004, p. 184):

Optimal efficiency in the use of class time

Development of self-management skills in students

Acceptable rate of appropriate student behavior

Use of positive motivational management techniques

Ability to cope with and remediate unexpected disruptions

Teaching responsibility also makes classes safer. Students cannot learn if they feel threatened or don't feel safe, emotionally or physically. Teaching students how to treat one another with respect makes the learning environment a nonthreatening and inviting place to move and learn.

It is a teacher's challenge to reach all students. Some of those students may have difficult home situations where they have few or no expectations to be responsible and respectable. Since the biggest reason for teaching responsible social behavior is for students to succeed, extra effort and patience may be needed to help these children. School may be the only place where they learn these skills.

Students need and want boundaries, and teaching responsibility can show them how to create their own boundaries. They learn that all their choices have a consequence, either good or bad, and those consequences create and teach the boundaries. If a student makes a poor choice and breaks some equipment, she will have nothing to play with. The student has learned that she needs to show respect to be able to play; the boundary has been set. In teaching responsible behavior, you are giving students the power to make good choices because it is the right thing to do, not because you are dangling a carrot in front them. This will empower them to develop self-management skills.

One of the most important life lessons we can teach our children is how to learn. Challenging oneself, setting goals, learning from mistakes, and persevering on the way to success can go a long way. An adult choosing to learn golf, whether for social or business reasons, has a better chance to be successful if he has learned how to challenge himself, set goals, learn from mistakes, and persevere. Learning any new skill later in life—technical, recreational, or academic—will be easier and faster if our students learn how to learn now.

There is no downside when you implement the levels and create a positive environment. Students are on task longer, so they become more successful; this leads to the enjoyment of movement and better skill acquisition. Students will make better lifestyle decisions when they enjoy and are successful in physical education. They will be lifelong movers!

Teaching Responsible Behavior in Physical Education

Physical education is uniquely positioned to effectively teach personal and social responsibility. Three of our six NASPE national standards address these positive behaviors (NASPE 2004):

○ The fifth standard says students should exhibit responsible personal and social behavior that respects self and others in physical activity settings. Our task as physical educators, then, is to teach our students what responsible behavior is and what respect for others and oneself looks and feels like. This is not a one day lesson; it is a lifetime of lessons. Every minute our students are in the gym, they are learning something about responsible and respectful behavior. We have the daunting task of making sure these are not wasted minutes.

○ The sixth standard says students should value physical activity for health, enjoyment, challenge, self expression, and social interaction. Two key points jump out: challenge and social interaction. The earlier students know how and why they should choose to challenge themselves, the better chance they have of reaching their potential. Setting goals and meeting challenges is key to success in life. Isn't this what all teachers want: that their students have a fulfilled life where they have become the best they can be? Furthermore, positive social interaction is an important factor in the development of children. We know there is a human need for touch and social interaction during the early stages of development and throughout a person's lifetime. It is our responsibility as educators to help our students obtain the social skills that will allow them to have positive social interactions for life.

○ The second standard states students should demonstrate understanding of movement concepts, principles, strategies, and tactics as they apply to the learning and performance of physical activities. In other words, we need to teach our students how to learn and practice effectively—to challenge themselves in order to improve their skills.

While other disciplines may have standards that touch on these areas, physical education has made them central to its goals. We have been assigned the charge to develop responsible children. In many ways, physical education is an integral part in the complete education of the whole child!

In the gym, students are often free to connect, communicate, and collaborate with their peers. During these interactions, students are making behavior choices that open the door to a wide range of learning opportunities. Add the sport requirement to follow rules, and you have a great recipe for learning responsible behaviors.

In competitive situations, students have the opportunity to practice self-control, honesty, respect, positive teamwork, and sportsmanship. Multiple teachable moments arise during games and station practice. We have the opportunity to teach conflict resolution, sportsmanship, and respect toward all.

Winning is not the only way to see oneself as successful. Goal setting is a wonderful tool for teaching success. Learning new skills, improving basic skills, and improving fitness scores are all great opportunities to teach goal setting. Without goals, how do we move forward towards success?

Teaching responsible behavior in a physical activity setting helps students learn through experience to accept differences in teammates and to work through conflict. They learn to show respect, to be honest, and to play by the rules. When goal setting is shown as a way to succeed, winning is put in perspective. They learn that they are responsible for their choices, and the consequences, both negative and positive, are theirs by choice. They become responsible citizens. We must take the initiative to use all our skills and resources to make physical education a place where the teaching and learning of responsible social behavior is effective.

Integrating the Levels With Your School's Programs

Most schools will have some type of character education program that teachers are to follow. NASPE standards and the three modified elementary levels fit well into these programs. One difference may be that often character education programs concentrate on one skill or value at a time, whereas we integrate the standards and the three modified elementary levels into every lesson. The levels will become the culture of your classroom.

You may have behavior models being used actively in your school. In my 20 years as an elementary physical education specialist, I have taken classes on cooperative discipline, tribes, and above the line philosophy and attended trainings in conscious discipline and the fish philosophy. They all share at least three features: Students choose their behavior, teachers need to make connections with their students, and teachers must be great positive communicators. In addition, most have a restorative component where students take the responsibility to make things right if a poor choice was made. Many have some type of conflict resolution addressed within the model. The three modified elementary levels work well with most of these philosophies. Table 1.1 shows a brief comparison of some models that your school may be using. It even includes one elementary school's mission statement to demonstrate how the levels can work with a mission statement as well.

Because teaching the three modified levels is an integrative approach, it's important to constantly be on the lookout for teaching opportunities. Hellison (2003) has five parts to a lesson: counseling time, awareness talk, the lesson, group meeting, and reflection. He is very aware of the time constraint of elementary specialists and says it may be difficult to get in the counseling time (which I refer to as making connections). You will need to put forth some effort in making connections with students during activity time, in the hallways, and before and after class. Included in this book are some resources that can be used for awareness talks—the children's stories and posters for what I call poster talks—that will teach your students about the three modified levels. Try to consistently take a few minutes at the end of class to talk about what the students learned during the lesson and about their responsible behavior choices. The group meeting and reflection time that Don Hellison describes will be your closure.

Teaching Responsible Behavior in Nonschool Environments

School is not the only environment where socially responsible behavior is taught. Camps, YMCAs, and community youth centers also share the goal of helping children reach their potential to become responsible, successful adults. Camps may stress environmental respect and responsibility along with teamwork and sportsmanship. Every environment has a unique opportunity to help children learn how to make good choices and how those choices will affect the world around them.

The YMCA has four core values: responsibility, respect, honesty, and caring. Teaching socially responsible behavior is a mission of the YMCA. The afterschool

TABLE 1.1 COMPARISON OF COMMON BEHAVIOR MANAGEMENT MODELS

Model	Description	Level 1 Respect	Level 2 Challenge	Level 3 Teamwork
Three modified elementary levels based on Don Hellison's model (Hellison 2003)	The three levels are intertwined and used daily. It is the culture of the gym. Clear expectations are consistently communicated. Students have choices. There is a small conflict resolution component. There is a restorative component. Children are taught to make good behavior choices. Intrinsic.	• Level 1 Respect	• Level 2 Challenge	• Level 3 Teamwork
Heritage Elementary Mission Statement: *Every person every day will learn, grow and help others to be respected and valued. Live it!*(Unified School District of De Pere 1996)	Mission statement was written by a committee of staff members when the school opened. It is taught by classroom teachers, and all children in the school know it. It teaches children to make good behavior choices.	• Respected and valued	• Every person, every day will learn and grow	• Help others • Valued
Tribes four agreements (Gibbs 2001)	Community is a key component. Community circles and team building activities are an important part of the program. The four agreements are the framework for working together. Students have choices. It is similar to cooperative discipline. It teaches children to make good behavior choices. Intrinsic.	• Attentive listening • Mutual respect	• Right to pass/right to participate	• No put-downs • Appreciation
Fish philosophy (Christensen, Halper, & Strand, 2006)	Based on the fishmongers of Pike Place Fish Market in Seattle. A key component is to play and have fun while being there for others and making their day. You are responsible for choosing your attitude, which affects your day and the people around you. Students have choices. Intrinsic.	• Choose your attitude	• Choose your attitude	• Make their day • Be there
Cooperative discipline (Albert,1996)	Helps the teacher see why students choose their behaviors and how they react to our responses. Connecting and collaborating are an emphasis. Students have choices. A restorative component is part of the model. It is similar to tribes. It teaches children to make good behavior choices. Intrinsic.	• Code of conduct	• Helps students feel capable • Mistakes are okay • Build confidence • Focus on successes • I can level • Recognize achievement	• Help students contribute • Help students connect Five relationships: • Acceptance • Attention • Appreciations • Affirmation • Affection
Conscious discipline (Bailey, 2001)	It helps the teacher see why students choose their behaviors and how they react to our responses. It helps students recognize their behavior, where it came from, and how to change it. Communicating expectations is a key component of conscious discipline. Conflict resolution is part of the model. A restorative component is part of the model. This teaches children to make good behavior choices. Intrinsic.	• Composure • Self-control • Consequences	• Choices	• Encouragement • Empathy • Positive intent

(continued)

TABLE 1.1 *(continued)*

Model	Description	Level 1 Respect	Level 2 Challenge	Level 3 Teamwork
Assertive discipline (Canter & Canter, 1996)	The teacher has power. It is based on teacher's needs. It includes assertive communication of expectations and behavior modification with rewards for good behavior. Controlling the student is the goal. Extrinsic.			
Above the line philosophy (Kronenberg, 1977)	Clear expectations that are consistent and constant. Three levels: • Above the line: Respect, responsibility, safety. • Below the line: Disrespect, irresponsibility. The teacher and student work out a plan to make it right. • Bottom of the line: Immoral, illegal, unsafe. The administration or police are involved in making it right. Teacher, students, staff have flexibility to add more behaviors above or below the line. There is a focus on student choice and a large restorative component. It is very similar to Hellison's levels of responsibility. It teaches children to make good behavior choices. Intrinsic.	• Respect and safety	• Responsibility	• No component but may be added by teacher or staff

program (for school-age children) and any of their youth programs can set the stage for teaching the core values through an emphasis on teamwork and sportsmanship.

Community youth centers need to make their centers a fun place to be. They want to get as many kids as they can into the center—a safe, nurturing environment—and off the streets. A youth center director I spoke with says the kids vote with their feet: If they walk into the center, it is a positive vote. To keep it fun, kids need to feel safe and accepted. For the center to be a safe and nurturing place where kids can have fun and be accepted, the kids will need to show respect. The community youth centers need and want to teach socially responsible behavior so they get a lot of feet walking through the door.

Summary

No matter our environment, we all have the responsibility to help kids be the best they can be. To do this, we need to join together and teach our children how to make good choices. Teaching them how to show respect, be responsible, challenge themselves, and accept everyone will give them the tools to make a difference in our world and in theirs. We can empower them to take charge of their behavior choices!

chapter 2

Creating a Positive Environment

Creating a positive environment at the beginning of the school year, on the very first day, is the best way to start the school year. Start by teaching the levels and then implement them into every class. The levels will become part of your teaching and contribute to the culture of your classroom. The levels will be woven into all of your lessons and units.

Implementing the Levels Is the Key

Remember, for students to be safe and ready to learn, Level 1 Respect will need to be demonstrated. You will need students to be at Level 1 Respect so instruction can take place, time will be used productively, and students will be safe both emotionally and physically. Level 1 Respect is crucial to every lesson. You and your students cannot be successful without it.

Your goal every day is to have students learn and grow in order to reach their potential. Level 2 Challenge will become an integral part of all your lessons. If you want your students to be successful, they will need to be challenged. Developing the *I can do* spirit from Level 2 Challenge will benefit your students for a lifetime. They will learn to take risks, make mistakes, and persevere. They will learn to focus, stay on task, and to change the task if it is too easy. They will become Challengers.

Having fun and making new friends will be the outcome of students demonstrating Level 3 Teamwork. Level 1 Respect and Level 2 Challenge will naturally be present in every lesson; Level 3 may need to be infused into them. Be creative and try to incorporate a Level 3 component into most of your lessons, depending on student maturity. They will learn the lifetime skill of collaboration and teamwork. They will become friends.

The resources included on the CD will help you implement the levels and build a positive environment. Posters will be visual reminders of the levels for both teacher and student. Students will know what each level looks and feels like by participating in the activities included in this book.

Using Common Language and Being Constantly Consistent

Using common language and being constantly consistent are the keys to successfully implementing the levels and creating a positive classroom environment. Constantly look for opportunities to talk about the levels using the common language of the levels and catch the students and class following them. Consistently expect your students to demonstrate the levels using the common language to state your expectations. I can't stress this enough. Your expectations and how you communicate them need to be consistent over time and setting.

When I refer to the common language, I'm talking about the terms you use consistently in class to refer to responsible behavior: it is simply using the language of the levels when you talk about behavior choices. If a student is talking while you are giving directions, you simply ask the student if she is at Level 1 Respect. You don't need to ask if she's paying attention, or ask her to please be quiet. If the class is talking, you simply say, "Level 1." Be consistent with your language choice and constantly look for opportunities to use it.

How you communicate is extremely important; keep it positive! Always ask positive questions so students think in the positive. "Are you at Level 1?" makes the student think, "What does Level 1 look like?" The student has a positive image. "Are you being a Friendly?" makes the student think of a Friendly and how he can care about others. If you question in the negative, you will be putting negative thoughts into developing brains. A poor question would be, "Are you being a Waster?" The student then thinks of what a Waster is and will identify himself with the Waster. Keep your communication positive. This will help your students' thoughts, choices, and actions stay positive.

Since the levels are interwoven into every lesson, you need to consistently have your students meet your expectations. If students think that you are not always going to expect them to make good choices, eventually they will stop making good choices. This will lead to frustration for both you and your students and a loss of precious learning time. Your expectations need to be consistent over time, place, students, and circumstance. This combination of being consistent through the use of positive common language and expectation of behavior and constantly looking for opportunities to teach the levels are the keys to your success and your student's growth.

In a classroom in which you have consistently communicated, constantly taught, and practiced your expectations, disruptions can easily be addressed by simple questioning:

What level are you at right now?

Would you like to change?

What do you need to do to change?

After a few friendly reminders through questioning if disruptions continue, students know the consequence is to sit by the Level 0 poster and reflect on their choice. When they are ready to *own the behavior* and agree to participate at Level 1 Respect, they may return to activity. With the system clearly communicated, taught, and practiced in a positive manner, less time is spent on disruptions.

There will still be an occasional big disruption that may take more time to address. Remember the student has made the behavior choice. Work with the student to help her to own the behavior and figure out how to make it right. This is a restorative action that should be part of working through any large disruption.

Use Procedures to Reinforce Learning

Class procedures are another aspect of creating a positive environment that should be consistent. Students need to know and practice the class procedures and management cues. Here are a few class procedures or management tricks that I incorporate to help build a positive environment.

To start class I have directions posted on the marker board for the warm-up of the day or a beginning instant activity. This not only gets students moving immediately, but it integrates reading skills and practice as well. Students learn to enter the gym and check the board for directions: they become engaged right away. The activity could be jogging, jumping rope, a team warm-up, jumping jacks on squad spots, or any instant activity that you have taught. Students who enter a gym and sit as the first activity are going to be less engaged and more likely to be disruptive.

I also organize the class so students know where to go for directions or warm-ups. I have squad spots painted on my gym floor. At the beginning of the year, students are assigned a squad spot. I use the pattern boy-girl-boy-girl and place students strategically according to their needs and behavior choices. At midyear I let the students choose their squad spots. I strategically place four to six students to start the boy-girl pattern and then let the rest of the students choose their squad spot. I can use these squads to divide the class into teams or stations groups or to quickly make dance or warm-up partners. Have your class organized in some manner to save time finding warm-up spots, choosing teams, or spreading out for active instruction.

I use *go words* and a *freeze routine* as consistent and reliable cues to indicate when students should move or stop moving and listen. We use a new go word every month. Students help pick these words. I'll start my directions with "When I say, 'blast off!' I would like you to walk and line up." No student should go until you say your go word. This keeps students stationary and attentive to directions until they are completely given. This will need to be practiced, and it will need to be used consistently to be effective.

To have students stop and freeze bodies, mouths, and equipment, I use the cue "Freeze! Thigh 5-4-3-2-1." On this cue, students should stop moving, equipment should be on the floor, and their hands should be on their thighs in a ready position. The backward count gives students a few extra seconds to respond, but they should not use all five seconds! This countdown gives the teacher a chance to scan the class. If the students do not freeze as directed, they are not at Level 1 Respect for rules, equipment, or teacher. Be consistent and give them a friendly reminder to be at Level 1.

To end the class, I have students walk to line up and sit in two lines. Always tell the students what the expectations are. For example, I might say, "When I say, 'Blast off,' please walk to the line and sit down." Be consistent; if a student runs and slides into the line, he should be asked to try to be at Level 1 again and practice walking to the line. While the students sit in line, review the skill of the day or their progress in obtaining the levels during class, your awareness talk. The quietest and straightest line leaves first. If there is a tie, pick a number for a student from each line to guess and closest goes first. Or use your own favorite tie-breaker.

Don't overlook how you transition your students. Well-planned transitions save time and get students active quickly. Fewer behavior problems occur when students are active and engaged. If I need to do a quick equipment change, I might ask my students to do shoulder touches or push-up soccer as I change the equipment. Or I might ask them to review the criteria for the skill they will be practicing with the person next to them in their squad. Being well prepared with thoughtful planning goes hand in hand with being consistent.

Be consistent in setting your students up for success. Designing lessons that are developmentally appropriate will help. Lesson design that allows for diverse learners keeps students engaged during activity. Design your lessons so the challenges you give your students can be made more or less challenging for your varied learners. You might have them change direction, speed, equipment, or side of body they are using. You can add a trick, more equipment, or more focus points to think about. My favorite is to change the number of trials or the distance of the challenge. I always plan to use a variety of equipment for the challenge. For example, I might have students choose from small and large objects to catch at the catching station. The section on making a challenge, in Teaching Level 2 Challenge, offers many more suggestions.

Connect, Communicate, and Collaborate

Connect, communicate, and collaborate was the convention theme of Jeff Lindauer, a past president of the Wisconsin Association of Physical Education, Health, Recreation and Dance. I have used this as a theme for creating a positive classroom environment.

Connecting with your students will build relationships. Students will be more successful if there is a bond between teacher and student. This connecting can happen with little gestures such as a thumb-up, a smile, or brief eye contact as you share your student's success. Building a connection through a gentle touch on the back as you give encouraging words shows you care when the going gets tough. Knowing your student's name helps with classroom management, but it also builds connections. Listening also builds relationships; listen attentively when a student excitedly tells you how he scored the winning goal single-handedly or lost a tooth. Sometimes it's the small things in life that add up to mean a lot.

Remember that communication should always be presented in a positive manner. Your actions will communicate a lot to your students. Make sure you demonstrate the three levels in your teaching. Communicate your expectations through the levels and demonstrate them through your actions.

Living the levels, talking about them daily, and catching the students following the levels and then giving specific positive feedback will motivate students to make good choices. Your positive feedback is a way to communicate with your students that you see their positive choices. This reinforcement helps the levels become natural. Because you have connected with your students, specific, positive feedback will mean more because they know you care.

Connect to your students; get to know their interests. Plan lessons in which students are engaged and learn to love to move! Activities need to be relevant and interesting to your students. You will keep them active, happy, and engaged by making connections and reflecting on your student's reaction to the activities you put before them. Students being actively engaged will make it less likely that they will make poor behavior choices.

Think of one of your favorite teachers: Did you feel connected? Chances are excellent the answer is yes. How did she build connections? Perhaps she gave you choices. One way to include choice is through collaboration. Do you set up stations that provide choices? Do you design lessons where the student can explore? Children grow by making decisions, learning from mistakes, and learning how to make choices. Level 2 Challenge helps with this collaborative aspect of a positive environment. It gives some power to the student in choosing how to challenge himself to learn and grow.

You might collaborate with students to eliminate a problem if there is a common recurring issue with a class, such as talking during directions. Bring the students together and open the discussion by asking if they have noticed the class having trouble showing Level 1 Respect to the teacher. Guide the students as they come up with a few solutions that might work. Students might suggest that they not sit with a friend, or that they should sit in squad order. Perhaps they'll decide that when the teacher raises one finger, it means they need to return to Level 1 Respect. Collaborate with your students to solve problems.

Students will also need to connect, communicate, and collaborate with their classmates. Giving students the opportunity to connect with all the students can be a challenge, but a noble one. The Common Mixer activity (page 122) in Teaching Level 3 Teamwork and the Every Child questionnaire (page 41) in Teaching Level 1 Respect are two ways to help students make connections to their classmates. Try to design lessons that allow students to work with friends but also forces them out of their comfort zone so they learn how to work with other classmates.

Teaching students how to give positive and specific feedback through the Challenge Coach activity in Teaching Level 2 Challenge will help teach them good communication (page 91). Expecting positive communication is great, but it works only if you have taught it so students know what it sounds like, feels like, and looks like. Students will need to learn how to communicate using praise phrases. There is a fun activity in Teaching Level 3 Teamwork to help students learn about praise phrases (page 125). Using the Levels to Solve Problems is a conflict resolution model (page 128) where communicating with classmates is an essential skill used to resolve disputes.

Students can collaborate while practicing partner skills, meeting group fitness challenges, solving team-building challenges, or creating games or routines. These are great opportunities for them to practice their communication skills. However, if everyone is not at the same level of good communication, a conflict will arise. Students should have some conflict resolution skills so the collaboration doesn't come to a standstill!

Obviously the teacher and students are the main characters who will create this positive environment. Your administration, other classroom teachers, and parents should have supporting roles. Remember to connect, communicate, and collaborate with them also.

Make a connection and set up a meeting with your administrator. Share with him the levels and their benefits through clear communication. Then collaborate; determine how you can team up to make the implementation of the levels successful.

The classroom teachers can be important allies. You might need to depend on their support when following up on behavior issues. Make a connection with them and communicate your classroom expectations. Hopefully this will help develop a collaborative relationship where the teachers reinforce the levels with your students in relation to physical education. For example, suppose a student was not at Level 1 Respect because they continuously did not freeze when asked. They sat out the last few minutes of class and missed their favorite activity. The student is pouting when the classroom teacher picks up the class. The classroom teacher is aware of the levels and reminds the student it was their choice not to freeze and perhaps should have chosen to be at Level 1. The next time the students come to class the classroom teacher has already reminded the student to be at Level 1 Respect for all of PE and that they will be very proud of them if they meet that goal!

Connect to your parents through clear communication. They need to know your expectations and the rationale behind them. Through this knowledge they will be able to support those expectations. The parent notes on the CD can lead to an informed collaborative relationship. Monthly or quarterly newsletters are another great way to communicate with parents about your great program. By attaching an activity calendar or log to your notes home, you are now collaborating with parents to help their children—your students—make healthy life style choices.

Positive Environments Outside of Physical Education

Where can these levels be used to help create a positive environment? Obviously the gym, but the classroom, playground, and entire school could benefit from the levels or the behaviors this book teaches and reinforces. The classroom teachers need to have respectful classrooms so instruction can take place, as well as a challenging atmosphere in which their students become shining stars. Many students learn cooperatively, so teamwork can also be an important element in a successful classroom.

In the gym when students are not at Level 1 after a few redirections, they have chosen to accept a consequence since they made the choice not to correct their behavior. The consequence may be sitting out and considering how they can change their behavior so they are at Level 1. This is a quick consequence. It has been predetermined and positively communicated. It is a natural, reflection-prompting consequence. They have been removed from activity so others can learn and be safe, or perhaps so equipment is not misused. They then have the opportunity to observe the correct behavior modeled by classmates. Students are allowed back in when they *own* their behavior and are ready to be at Level 1. The classroom teacher will need to decide what an appropriate quick, natural, and reflective consequence is for a student who is not at Level 1 Respect. Remember, however, that a major disruption will need to have a restorative component where the student collaborates with the teacher to decide how to make things right.

The playground is so similar to the physical education setting it would be quite easy to implement the three elementary levels. Consistent rules and expectations help students make good choices, hopefully producing fewer arguments between students. Consistent rules can refer not only to expectations but also the rules of the games played on the playground. Make sure all game rules are communicated clearly so every student knows how to play the games fairly.

Since there is less supervision on the playground, students have the chance to apply what they have learned in physical education. It is a great place for students to demonstrate respect for rules by being honest. With less supervision, arguments may be more frequent, so make sure students can resolve conflicts with Rock-Paper-Scissors or by referring to the process Using the Levels to Solve Problems on the CD (Level 3 Teamwork\Posters). Other conflict resolution strategies can also be taught.

The levels have a valuable contribution to make to community centers. I once had the pleasure of meeting with the director of a local community youth center. My first impression as I toured the facility was that of awe. There were so many children from so many different backgrounds actively involved in being a child. Choice was whispering in all their ears: choices to play a game, to surf the Web, to go to the gym, to become an artist or a musician, to be with a friend, to become a leader. All these choices build skills—academic, social, technical—that will help them reach their potential. Perhaps they will find their passion within the sea of choices that can lead to a fulfilling career choice.

Some of the children come from homes that lack a positive environment. The youth center exists to provide such an environment. I saw connections being made between staff and youth. Through their choices, students were empowered to collaborate. The levels, and especially the concepts in the stories and the accompanying activities, could be used as a tool to communicate to the young people how their choices can lead them to become the best they can be.

Camps are very active places where incorporating the levels could help keep campers safe. Safety around lakes, while hiking, and at camp fires is imperative to a good camp program. Simply using the story "Who Wears Gym Shoes? A Respectaroo" would set the groundwork for young campers to understand the meaning of respect. After the story has been read, discuss what being safe around camp would look like. Each letter of RESPECT can be tweaked to represent the camp environment. Respecting equipment would include the recreational equipment and craft supplies, along with boats and canoes. Nature could be looked upon as another type of equipment that deserves respect. Or perhaps nature could be seen as an extension of every child, the diversity of living things. Brainstorm with the campers what respect to nature would look like.

My good friend Terry, who was the music teacher at my school, is trying an adaptation of the three modified elementary levels. We were brainstorming how she could adapt them for her music classroom and chose the three levels of Respect, Risk-Taking, and Harmony. She often asks her students to take risks, thus the risk-taking level; it is common language her students are familiar with. Living in Harmony had a musical twist for the social teamwork level. After some thought, she decided to use the common language found in her school's mission statement for her levels. Terry developed her levels into Be Kind (Teamwork), Be Safe (Respect) and Be Your Best (Challenge). Whatever methods or processes you use to create a positive classroom environment, remember to make it your own. It needs to fit you, your students, and your school community.

Summary

It's important to make our classroom environment a safe, positive place where kids want to be and want to learn. Implement the levels at the beginning of the year and reinforce them daily. Use positive common language while always remembering to be consistent and constantly look for opportunities to teach the levels. Design lessons that are developmentally appropriate and differentiated for all learners. Organize your class so students transition efficiently by knowing your classroom management procedures and cues. Connect, communicate, and collaborate with students, parents, teachers, and administrators. This is the path to creating a learning culture in your classroom and a positive, safe environment in which to learn.

chapter 3

Assessing Students (and Yourself)

Assessment is not just a check for student learning; it is also a way for teachers to check how effective their teaching is. We assess our students, and we should also assess ourselves and our lesson designs. Just as we ask our students to reflect at the end of class or within an assessment, we need to reflect as well. Implementing the levels can extend to reflecting on your teaching: Ask yourself if the lesson you presented will make your students feel respected. Will all students feel challenged during the lesson? Are you setting up your students for success to demonstrate teamwork with their classmates? These are questions that could be asked with every lesson and activity.

Assessing Yourself

As you read this book, I hope you are getting a sense for how these levels and activities have evolved over the years. This would not have happened if I had not reflected on my teaching and assessed my own lesson design. Here are two of the most important questions you need to ask: What do you want your students to know, and how will you know they learned it? Good lesson design, based on standards and solid assessment showing what students are learning or have learned, will be your outcome. If you become a self-reflective teacher who sets challenges for yourself, positive outcomes will be your reward.

It is important to demonstrate what you want your students to learn. You need to show them respect. Make connections and learn who your students are. If you are respectful when students make poor choices, you can choose how to handle the incident. Challenge yourself to be the best teacher you can be. Attend workshops and collaborate with other professionals. Reflect on your lessons and assessments. Take risks, try new skills, and implement the three modified elementary levels.

After you teach a lesson, reflect on it and see if you want to incorporate something new the next time you teach the skill or concept. Remember to challenge yourself and assess your own teaching. Model for your students: "Challenge, challenge, that's the way to go; then you can learn and grow."

Some teaching situations involve team teaching. Use teamwork to help coworkers think about their teaching. Your example of being a self-reflective teacher is a great way to start. Share your ideas and experiences and listen to your coworkers' ideas. Together plan well-designed lessons that make all children feel respected when they stay active and challenged. Help your colleagues become better teachers so more students benefit.

Assessment Tools

Since we are responsible for teaching and assessing a variety of skills, appropriate assessment tools are essential. Both formal and informal assessments can be valid if used correctly. The most widely used formal assessment in physical education is fitness testing. High school physical education teachers may give a written test as an assessment at the end of a unit, but this type of formal assessment is not as common in elementary physical education, where performance rubrics are a more common type of formal assessment. With a formal assessment you can examine student's scores to see where they fall within a range of scores.

This book includes three rubrics, one for each of the three modified elementary levels. Students should be able to look at these rubrics and understand the expectations. They are in line with instruction principles and the national standards. The rubrics list the behaviors expected as criteria. The student needs to demonstrate all the behaviors to meet expectations. The rubrics are shown in tables 3.1-3.3.

Some of the homework activities included on the CD could be used as formal assessments because they were designed for reflection and reinforcement of concepts. For younger students there are two homework assignments: In one they draw a picture, and in the other they draw a line to the picture that shows the correct behavior choice. For older students the object of the homework is to apply what they have learned in physical education to situations outside of the gym. Any of these could be used as an assessment tool to monitor a student's progress toward mastering the levels.

Informal Assessments

Assessment can have two foci. One is to check what the students have learned. We use *summative,* or *formal, assessment* to check what the student has learned and then use it to assign a grade. The other focus is determining if students are learning what we want them to, identifying where in the process they are at the time. This is *formative,* or *informal, assessment*. After a formative assessment, the self-reflective teacher will use the information she obtained to make adjustments on the spot in her lesson, or design a new lesson as needed. How often do we use formative assessment to check for learning and then adapt our teaching? Many of us use informal assessments to help us with this question.

Much can be learned from informal assessments, such as where the student is in the process of becoming secure in the skill or concept. Observation is the informal assessment most physical education professionals master first. We are constantly observing and assessing and then giving positive specific feedback to our students. A majority of our informal assessment is through observation, but there are other

TABLE 3.1 RESPECT RUBRIC

Level 1 Respect	Criteria
Beginning Demonstrates 0 or 1 of the criteria	Shows respect for rules by honestly following them Shows respect for equipment by using it the correct way and putting it away when done
Developing Demonstrates 2 or 3 of the criteria	Shows respect for self and others by playing safely Shows respect for people and every child by being kind, taking turns, sharing, and not interfering
Meets expectations Demonstrates all of the criteria	Shows respect for teacher by listening attentively and follows directions Takes responsibility for personal behavior
Exceeds expectations Demonstrates all of the criteria Helps others follow rules Sees unsafe situations and tries to correct them Uses praise phrases	

TABLE 3.2 CHALLENGE RUBRIC

Level 2 Challenge	Criteria
Beginning Demonstrates 0 or 1 of the criteria	Practices, practices, practices until the teacher signals the end Works independently and thinks, thinks, thinks while practicing
Developing Demonstrates 2 or 3 of the criteria	Challenges self without the teacher's reminders Tries new movements and skills willingly Participates even when not successful
Meets Expectations Demonstrates all of the criteria	
Exceeds Expectations Demonstrates all of the criteria Helps others to challenge themselves Challenges self outside of physical education	

TABLE 3.3 TEAMWORK RUBRIC

Level 3 Teamwork	Criteria
Beginning Demonstrates 0 or 1 of the criteria	Tries not to argue and uses acceptable conflict resolution during class Regularly encourages others and doesn't use put-downs
Developing Demonstrates 2 or 3 of the criteria	Cooperates with all class members by taking turns and sharing equipment Is a friend to all Helps others solve problems or meet challenges
Meets expectations Demonstrates all of the criteria	
Exceeds expectations Demonstrates all of the criteria Initiates play with a classmate who is left out of a group	

quick informal assessments that help us gather information on our students and our teaching.

Questioning during class is probably the most common informal assessment I use other than observation. Simply asking a student if he is working at Level 2 Challenge when off task can bring the student back to Level 2. You quickly see where the student is in the process of controlling his choices to help him become a challenger.

This book and CD include several other informal assessment ideas and resources you can use. Here are a few of my favorites.

Touch Poster

One of the informal assessments I use in checking what level students feel they were at during class is to have students touch the levels chart (on the CD in the All Levels folder) on the way out of the gym (Hellison, 2003 page 52). Most students should be touching both Level 1 Respect and Level 2 Challenge at the end of class. If students were working with a partner or in groups, or playing a cooperative game, they should also be touching Level 3 Teamwork as well. Level 0 is posted on the chart also.

It is a good idea to spot-check this process. I watch what levels the students touch and reinforce their choice. There are times I question whether they are being honest with themselves and ask them to think about what happened during class, re-evaluate, and then touch the chart again. This is a quick, thought-provoking assessment that takes little time.

Thumbs-Up

A thumbs-up appraisal is another quick informal assessment you can use during class. A thumbs-up signal from the teacher means the level was reached for most of the class. A thumbs-to-the-side signals the level was reached sometimes during the class, and thumbs-down means better choices next time are in order. The thumb assessment can be used with any of the three levels. This assessment can be done at the end of class as a closure activity. It can also be used in the middle of class as a way for students to evaluate what level they are at and decide if changes need to be made. Perhaps students are having trouble putting away equipment between stations. A quick thumbs assessment may help students get back to Level 1 Respect for equipment. Both the touch poster and thumbs-up check informal assessment ideas are also in Hellison's book *Teaching Responsibility Through Physical Activity* (2003).

Graphing

Another great informal assessment method is *graphing*. It is a good way to see where students are in the process of acquiring the skill of demonstrating respect, challenging themselves, using teamwork, and understanding the effects of individual choice.

Level touch chart.

The graph I use for assessing respect can be made with the RESPECT graph pieces on the CD (under Level 1 Respect in the Reflection subfolder). I put the letters across the top of a pocket chart and print and laminate the Respectaroo graph pieces to use on the chart. You can also create a Respectaroo mascot to hold the graph pieces—I bought a stuffed Kangaroo and dressed it in tennis shoes, a red baseball cap, and a t-shirt from a local make-your-own-stuffed-animal store and put the graph pieces in the Respectaroo's pouch.

Bring the students together and ask them to give examples of how they showed respect for rules. If possible let the student put the Respectaroo graph piece in the pocket chart under the letter R. Perhaps two or three students will give examples. Then go next to the letter E for equipment and ask for examples of how the class showed respect for equipment. Continue through all the letters and help the class summarize what they see from the graph. As you or a student add Respectaroo graph pieces, students will have a literal image of where the class' strengths and weaknesses are.

The graphing activity can be flexible. For example, when I use the pocket chart in my dance unit, we may just graph the letter P for people and EC for every child. In a review setting after a period when students were not freezing and were playing with equipment during directions, I may graph just R (rules), E (equipment), and T (teacher). If a quick review of Level 1 Respect is needed, the pocket chart can be pulled out. In the beginning, I left mine on a cart that held my CD player. I could hang it quickly on my marker board with clips. I found myself using the graph system more, and now I have my pocket chart hanging on the wall near the door where we line up. This system works well at the beginning of the year to help reinforce Level 1 Respect. It will help you assess the students' progress in grasping the concept of respect.

The Level 2 Challenge graph on the CD (under Level 2 Challenge in the Reflection subfolder) is based on what a challenger does: Think, practice, and make a task a challenge if it is too easy. Place the challenger graph pieces under the correct heading. This graph is great when doing the Challenge Coach activities or when students are learning a new skill. It is also useful when students are engaged at fitness stations that require proper technique or are working through the jump rope unit.

The Level 3 Teamwork graph (on the CD under Level 3 Teamwork in the Reflection subfolder) is used in a slightly different manner. After reading the story "Who Will You Be in PE?" we review what a Friendly does. As the students name the quality of a Friendly, I put the corresponding graph

From S. Hagenbach, 2011, *Teaching children responsible behavior: A complete toolkit* (Champaign, IL: Human Kinetics).

Graph pieces for assessing respect.

From S. Hagenbach, 2011, *Teaching children responsible behavior: A complete toolkit* (Champaign, IL: Human Kinetics).

Graph pieces for assessing challenge.

Shares
Takes turns
Is helpful
Is polite
Compromises

From S. Hagenbach, 2011, *Teaching children responsible behavior: A complete toolkit* (Champaign, IL: Human Kinetics).

Graph pieces for assessing teamwork.

piece in the pocket chart. Over the next few classes, as we do the various Friendly activities, we place a Friendly graph piece next to the quality we practiced.

You can also use the Friendly graph to prepare students for a cooperative activity. Place the qualities on which you want the students to concentrate while they are participating in a cooperative activity in the pocket chart. Discuss these qualities before the activity, and review the graph afterward.

Be a self-reflective teacher and use what you learn to make adjustments to your teaching. Remember that assessment is not only used to see what the student knows but should also be used to guide your teaching.

Word Wall

A word wall discussion at the end of class can be used to bring closure to the lesson and to give the students a little time to decompress and calm down. Each year I put up a word wall with a special theme where I can post the key skills and concepts students learn throughout the year. These words act as learning targets for my class. At the end of class, students form two lines facing the word wall, and we do a quick question-and-answer session. I ask a few questions about the key word, for example, *underhand throw*. The student wishing to answer the question must catch an object that I toss. You can also incorporate questions about the level choices they made for the day while reviewing the key word. An example of this questioning might be "What level were you when you were thinking about taking an opposite-foot step?" The closure at the end of class can be both on the students' level choices and a review of the key skills taught. This is another good example of an informal assessment that integrates reading through the use of a word wall, as well as one that helps the teacher assess where his students are in the process of acquiring skills and concepts.

Smile! Peer Assessment

A quick paper-and-pencil assessment can work well with older students to evaluate each other. After a partner dance or team activity, students put the name of the partner they are evaluating on a scrap of paper and use the following rating scale to evaluate that partner's demonstration of respect:

Smiley—My partner showed me respect most of the time.

Straight face—My partner showed me respect some of the time.

Frown—My partner did not make me feel respected.

This evaluation happens periodically, once or twice over the course of the unit.

The first time I used this system I maintained notes on students who did well and students who were having difficulty; I wanted to make sure that students weren't showing favoritism to their friends in evaluations, and comparing my notes with theirs helped me gauge the validity of their feedback. I used this information to put a level grade in the grade book if I deemed it valid. I did mark it as a peer evaluation and not a teacher evaluation. It helped me to see where students were in the process of being able to accept all peers without regard to personal differences and in working productively with a partner or in small groups.

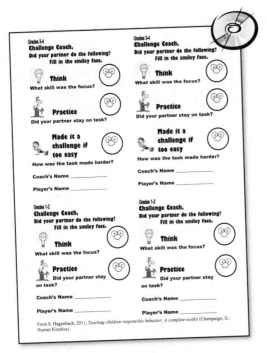

Challenge Coach assessment.

The Challenge Coach assessment is a smiley face fill-in. This assessment could be used with second through fourth grades. There are three questions that the challenge coach is asking while the player is practicing. Is the player thinking about the skill? Is she practicing and staying on task for the allotted time? Is she making the task into a challenge if it is too easy? Younger students would just answer the first two questions, while older students ask all three questions. The assessment is on the CD (under Level 2 Challenge in the Activities subfolder).

Self-Assessment

"How am I doing?" is a great question students may ask themselves. The CD includes two simple self-assessments that can be used with primary and upper-level students. The primary assessment instructs students to fill in a smiley face with a grin if they were at the level most of the time, a straight face if they are at the level some of the time, and a frown if they could improve on the choices they make. The upper level assessment is a check list. (Both files are on the CD in the All Levels folder.) Students put a + next to the statement if it is what they demonstrate most of the time, a √ if the statement is what they do sometimes, and a – if they need to improve.

Assessment as Communication

Assessment is also used as a form of communication with both the parents and the students. A major communication tool is the report card. We are responsible for giving grades that are based on documented observations, not our feelings. The following is a summary of my class expectations followed by a notation system that will help you communicate with parents and students. Parents are informed at the beginning of the year in an introductory letter about the three levels used in physical education (in the All Levels folder; also see page 27). Students are taught the expectations at the beginning of the year and then these are reinforced daily. Students are expected to demonstrate Level 1 Respect during class, to aspire to reach Level 2 Challenge when moving, and to strive for Level 3 Teamwork whenever possible.

Keeping track of student behavior for assessment reasons can be a daunting task. I have developed a quick and easy system to track student behavior, based on the RESPECT acrostic. These notes and anecdotal records help me assign at least one weekly grade. Long written notes are not necessary with this easy notation system—you just need to keep the grade book handy! This system is very helpful when communicating with parents and students at conferences and when giving grades.

Communicate with your students that you will be keeping little notes to help them see how their decisions affect their learning. Share your findings with students periodically. Remind them that all the notations are based on their choices. Using this notation system will reinforce good choices and hopefully help some students to make better choices if necessary.

Behaviors that are not a level 1 are noted as level 0. I use the following key:

R—students not following class rules or game rules

E—students not using equipment appropriately

S—students not being safe

P—student not showing respect to people

T—students not showing respect to the teacher, talking during directions

I will sometimes combine two letters and circle them. For example, if a student is not being safe with a classmate, I would put a circled SP in the grade book by that student's name. Or if a student continues to play with equipment on a "Freeze," I

How Are You Doing assessment for grades K-2

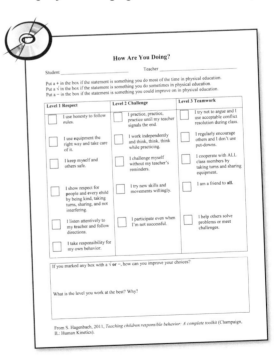

How Are You Doing assessment for grades 3-4

Dear Parents or Guardians,

Physical education is more than learning skills, getting your heart pumping, and playing games. It involves the development of the whole child. As your child's physical education teacher, I want to help instill the value of respect, the satisfaction of success that comes from being challenged, and the wonder of teamwork.

Our students will be learning about making positive choices that will affect themselves and others in physical education in three areas: respect, challenge, and teamwork. These areas, or levels, are based on Don Hellison's model detailed in the book *Teaching Responsibility Through Physical Activity*. They have been modified for elementary students by Sandy Hagenbach and are based on our national standards for physical education.

One of our national standards addresses respectful behavior. Standard 5 states students will exhibit responsible personal and social behavior that respects self and others in physical activity settings. **Level 1 Respect** teaches students to respect **r**ules, **e**quipment, **s**elf, **p**eople, **e**very **c**hild, and **t**eacher. Students who show Level 1 Respect will help make their physical education class a place where everyone can learn and be safe.

The second national standard addresses the learning and performance of physical activities. The book *Moving Into the Future: National Standards for Physical Education* offers two examples of outcomes related to this standard:

- A student can state that best effort is shown by trying new or hard tasks.
- A student can explain that appropriate practice improves performance.

Level 2 Challenge helps teach students that, to learn and grow, they need to challenge themselves. Reaching their potential is the emphasis.

Level 3 Teamwork also helps achieve standard 5. Outcomes relevant to this standard state that students will

- accept all playmates without regard to personal differences,
- work productively with a partner to improve performances, and
- regularly encourage others and refrain from put-downs.

Younger students will learn that teamwork is helping others solve problems or meet challenges. Older students will explore what teamwork is through cooperative activities and discover that teamwork involves respect, challenge, communicating, and planning. Teamwork helps make games more fun for everyone.

These levels are interrelated. You cannot have great teamwork without respect and challenge. Students will be expected to be at Level 1 Respect to participate in physical education. Friendly reminders and redirection will help students make good choices. High expectations yield great outcomes. I look forward to watching your child learn and grow both physically and socially through the year. If you have any questions concerning your child's physical education experience, please contact me.

Sincerely,

Parent level letter.

would put a circled RE in the grade book for that student.

Students off-task who are not at Level 2 Challenge are noted at Level 1. For example, a student who is not doing a warm-up with effort, would have a 1w (the *w* stands for warm-up) in the grade book. Students off-task at stations—not practicing the skill of the day—would be noted with a 1s (the *s* stands for skill).

Put any grades that are 0 or 1 in the grade book as soon as possible if the behavior is worth noting, or you may forget. If a student sits out, I try to put a level grade in the grade book.

Students going beyond the normal effort expected in class can have a 2+ noted in the grade book.

When group work is not a focus, or a student shines at Level 3 Teamwork, a 3 is noted in the grade book. For example, the following behaviors would merit a 3:

○ Student helps another student with directions.

○ Student helps teacher pick up some equipment without being asked.

○ Student invites another student into the group.

○ The teacher may need to have someone leave a group and work with another student and a student willingly leaves her group to help someone out.

○ During a game, the student shares consistently.

If nothing is noted, and a teamwork grade was not given during a group focus lesson, the student will achieve a Level 2 grade for the week.

Here is a quick review on the notation system:

0 with key letter—Student not showing Level 1 Respect

1—Student off-task, not at Level 2 Challenge

2—Student showing Level 1 Respect and at Level 2 Challenge

2+—Student showing extra effort

3—Student working at Level 3 Teamwork when group work is not the focus

A sample grade book illustrating the notation system is shown on page 29. Looking at these sample pages it is easy to see that Jim Shue needs to improve his Level 2 Challenge. Jack Jumpin probably likes to talk during directions. Anita Job demonstrates Level 3 Teamwork and probably works with a variety of people willingly. Ben Jamin challenges himself and puts in extra effort. Roger Wilko needs to make better choice and has trouble working at Level 1 Respect. Jim Shorts needs to put more effort into warm-ups and has difficulty working with people at Level 1 Respect. Otto Field needs to participate more safely. Rhonda World, Crystal Waters, Tom Turkey, Anny Player, Mark Deball, Sunny Court, and Holly Bush consistently work at Level 1 Respect, Level 2 Challenge, and when asked, Level 3 Teamwork.

Communication with parents takes place at other times during the year besides report card time: conferences, newsletters, and emails are a few examples of these added events. The De Pere elementary physical education team wanted to develop a communication tool to be used at any time during the year to inform parents of the progress their children were making with social skills. I designed the tool and adapted it for my levels. There are two notes; they include a simple rubric that could be sent to parents—one for a student who is excelling and one for a student who may be struggling. These progress reports are on the CD, in the All Levels folder.

BEHAVIOR ASSESSMENT SAMPLE

Name													
Beach, Sandy	1w	SP	2+										
Bush, Holly													
Court, Sunny													
Deball, Mark													
Field, Otto	S	SE	SP	S	S								
Jamin, Ben	2+	3	3	2+	2+								
Job, Anita	2+	3	3	3	2+	3							
Jumpin, Jack	T	T	T	3									
Moeney, Sarah	3	3											
Player, Anny													
Shorts, Jim	P	1w	T	1w	RE	SP	P	1w	P				
Shue, Jim	1w	1w	1s	1w	1s								
Turkey, Tom													
Waters, Crystal													
Wilko, Roger	R	E	R	T	P	1s	E	RE	RE				
World, Rhonda													

Summary

It takes time to incorporate any teaching tool into a teacher's repertoire. Make the new tools you use your own and then adapt and use them. Remember to be consistent. Use both informal and formal assessments to discover where your students are in the learning process and what they have learned. Use this information to make yourself a better teacher and your students better Challengers.

Assessment should help drive your instruction. Start your lesson design with an assessment that will show whether your students have reached the desired outcome. Use informal assessment throughout the unit, lesson, or activity to see where your students are in the process of reaching this outcome. Remember that assessment is for both teachers and students. Students can see if they are on target to reach the specified outcome and know when they have met it. Teachers can reflect on their teaching through assessment and then use these reflections as a guide to improve instruction.

PART II

Unit Plans for Teaching Responsible Behavior

Respect

Teaching young children a new concept involves helping them to see, feel, and experience it. Having students see, feel, and experience respect as it relates to the physical education setting can be challenging. With the use of an acrostic, the illustrated children's story "Who Wears Gym Shoes? A Respectaroo," and some fun activities, students will be able to learn about respect and make positive personal choices in physical education.

Children's Story

"Who Wears Gym Shoes? A Respectaroo" is a rhyming story that uses an acrostic to teach what respect looks like. (An acrostic is a memory aid. In this case it uses each letter of the word *respect* to represent a longer phrase.) The main character is a happy, active kangaroo who wears gym shoes. The story appears on page 55 of this book and is also on the CD (Level 1 Respect\Story).

Each letter of the word RESPECT stands for something that students should respect in the gym:

R represents respecting **r**ules. You need to follow them honestly.

E represents respecting **e**quipment. You need to take care of it.

S represents respecting one's **s**elf. You need to be safe and active.

P represents respecting **p**eople. You need to be a friend.

EC represents respecting **e**very **c**hild, keeping him safe, staying calm, and not going wild. (For older students, I expand the E to include all children, no matter how they look, what abilities they have, what they own, how old they are, or if they are boys or girls.)

T represents respecting the **t**eacher. You need to listen and follow directions.

As you read this story, point out how each letter of the word *respect* stands for something. Let your students know an acrostic is a memory tool they can use to help them remember what respect looks like.

Who Wears Gym Shoes?

A Respectaroo!

Sandy Hagenbach

"Who Wears Gym Shoes? A Respectaroo" is on page 55 and the CD.

This story can be used with kindergarten through second grade to introduce or reinforce the concept of respect or Level 1 Respect. A beginning-of-the-year bulletin board could be created from the pages of the story. Remind students showing respect is a choice they make.

For people who work in a YMCA setting, you might point out that Level 1 Respect reinforces three of the core values. The core value of respect is clear. Respect for rules is related to the core value of honesty. Taking care of equipment reinforces the core value of responsibility.

Introducing Level 1 Respect

The first day that the concept of respect is introduced to primary students, kindergarten, and first grade, I read the story or show the PowerPoint of "Who Wears Gym Shoes? A Respectaroo." If time is a concern, and you have made connections with the classroom teacher, the classroom teacher could read the story right before she brings her students to physical education class. Have the gym prearranged with a variety of equipment—hula hoops, playground balls, jump ropes, objects for catching, and lowered baskets, if possible—placed around the gym. It will be used in an activity to help students practice showing respect.

After the story, introduce the *freeze* and *go word* concepts. Explain how the class can show respect for rules and the teacher by freezing when asked. My method is to say, "Freeze! Thigh 5-4-3-2-1." Students put equipment on the floor and place their five fingers (hand) on their thighs. On a good freeze, there should be no movement by the time I count down to 3 or 4. Counting down gives me time to catch them doing the freeze correctly or redirect students who need help. It works well, and it only took me 20 years to figure it out!

Next, explain the go word. The go word is a cue to students that they may *unfreeze* and move according to teacher instructions. For example, before giving instructions, start your sentence with, "When I say *blastoff*, I'd like you to . . . ." It will take some practice. If I don't start the instructions with the request to wait for the go word, students are likely to follow the instructions right away.

Students can choose a new go word each month. I always start September with the go word *blastoff*. I practice this frequently while practicing Level 1 Respect. I also try to trick them in a manner similar to Simon Says. In January, the word chosen by the students may be *snowstorm*. I may call out *snowshoe* just to see if they are listening. It keeps the students on their toes. Using a go word prevents students from moving before you are finished with directions and helps them listen attentively.

Explain that they can play with any equipment as long as they show respect and take care of it. They need to show respect to themselves by being safe and active and towards people and every child by being a friend to all. When you say, "Freeze! Thigh 5-4-3-2-1" or turn off the music, they must stop, put down equipment with hands on their thighs, and wait for directions. Catch them being at Level 1 Respect. Students may then go to new equipment.

If there's time, I also play "The Freeze Dance" by Greg and Steve, found on their *Kids in Motion* CD. It is a great song that stops intermittently on the word *freeze*. This reinforces the *Freeze Thigh 5* concept.

For second and third grades, a possible first lesson could consist of reviewing the concepts of the story with a poster talk, learning the Respect chant, doing the

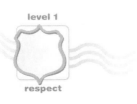

level 1

respect

From S. Hagenbach, 2011, *Teaching children responsible behavior: A complete toolkit* (Champaign, IL: Human Kinetics).

Respect poster talk letters for grades 2-3.

Respect Dance, and then playing Respect Tag, all of which are described in the following pages.

The poster talk for second and third graders is a chart of ways to show Level 1 Respect. I take seven large pieces of paper in different colors and post one letter on each of the sheets. You can find the letters on the CD (Level 1 Respect\Posters\ Respect Poster Talk 2-3). These letters do not have any cues on them. In a class discussion, talk about different ways to show respect for each of the letters of the acrostic. Introduce the concept of E for Every person. Explain that all people deserve respect, no matter how they look, what they own, how old they are, what their abilities are, or if they are boys or girls. List the students' ideas of how to show respect on the large pieces of paper.

○ RESPECT DANCE AND CHANT

Movement and dance are great ways to help students remember concepts. You may want to teach this dance and then add the Respect Chant: "Rules-Equipment-Self-People-Every Child-and the Teacher." The dance is appropriate for late kindergarten through fourth grade. The dance with the chant is appropriate for late second grade through fourth grade.

Do the following steps to Aretha Franklin's song "Respect":

You may add the following chant to the 16-count slides that change every 4 counts. Then you may speed up the chant for the next 8 counts where the arm motion changes to every 2 counts:

"Rules, Equipment, Self, People, Every Child, and the Teacher."

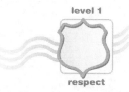

level 1

respect

16 ct	Intro music: Step close R-L-R-L
16 ct Jump pattern	2 jumps left, 2 jumps right, 2 jumps left, 2 jumps right Arms high, punch to opposite corner as you jump (may add chant*)
8 ct Jump patterrn	Punch arms: Left high, right high, left low, right low every two counts (may add chant)
16 ct Jump pattern	8 jumping jacks or raise the roof**
16 ct + 8 ct + 16 ct 2 more times	Do **jump pattern** with arm punch two more times (may add chant) 16 ct 2 jumps left, 2 jumps right, 2 jumps left, 2 jumps right Arms high, punch to opposite corner as you jump 8 ct punch arms: Left high, right high, left low, right low every two counts 16 ct 8 jumping jacks or raise the roof
32 ct	Jog (You may turn and face a different direction every 8 ct)
16 ct + 8 ct + 16 ct	Do **jump pattern** with arm punch (may add chant)
16 ct	Punch arms: Left high, right high, left low, right low every count "R-E-S-P-E-C-T"
32 ct	Roll arms like punching bag and jog or pony step. "Sock it to me" (You may turn and face a different direction every 8 ct)
16 ct	Step close R-L-R-L to end

*Chant—"Rules–Equipment–Self–People–Every Child and the Teacher"
**Raise the roof—High knee lift and hop while pushing hands up over head, then switch to opposite knee.

○ RESPECT TAG

Equipment

▶ 6 dice cards (on the CD, Level 1 Respect\Activities\Respect Tag). I have two dice with clear pockets on all sides into which I place the cards. If you don't have pocket dice, you could tape the cards to a die or mount the tag cards on a wall and assign corresponding numbers that students would use when rolling a standard die.

▶ 2 deck rings for taggers representing Level 0

▶ 3 to 6 balls

▶ 1 or 2 targets such as a laundry basket

▶ 15 to 20 bean bags in a container

▶ Some cones or poly spots to mark off the "show respect, get back in" area

▶ The song "Respect" from Aretha Franklin to start and stop the game

Description

Students are scattered with one or two taggers. Depending on the students' skill level, you may have your students gallop and slide instead of run during the tag game. Remind them to show respect for the rules by being honest. If they fall down, crash, or go out of bounds, they must send themselves to the "show respect, get back in" area. If they are tagged by a Level 0 tagger, they must also go to the "show respect, get back in"

area. When in the "show respect, get back in" area, students roll the dice and follow the directions to re-enter the game:

The following are the dice card directions:

▶ Rules: Be honest. Throw three balls into the target without stepping over the line.

▶ Equipment: Put it away and do not play. Pick up three beanbags and put them away.

▶ Self: Be active and be safe. Do 10 jumping jacks without hitting anyone.

▶ People: Be a friend. Give two people a high five.

▶ Every Child: Include every child and don't go wild. Safely find a person you do not play with often and tell him something nice.

▶ Teacher: Listen to her and follow directions. Tell the teacher what each letter in the word respect stands for (the chant from the dance): rules, equipment, self, people, every child, and the teacher.

Rules
Toss 3 balls into the target from behind the line.
Play fair. Be honest.
Follow the rules.

Equipment
Pick up 3 beanbags and put them in the container.
Put it away. Take care of it.
Use it the right way.

Self
Find a safe spot and do 5 jumping jacks.
Be safe.   Be active.

People
Give 3 people a gentle high-five.
Be a friend.   Share and care.

From S. Hagenbach, 2011, *Teaching children responsible behavior: A complete toolkit* (Champaign, IL: Human Kinetics).

Respect Tag dice cards.

Once the task described on the die is completed, students may return to the game. Students enjoy learning the chant. It is a fun challenge, like learning to say *supercalafragilisticexpialadocious.* See who can say the respect chant the fastest!

First graders may need some reminders on what the activity is for each card. Most second graders should be able to read the directions. I do not use this game with kindergarteners at the beginning of the year.

Reinforcing Level 1 Respect

For kindergarten and first grade students, I review the acrostic on the second day with the use of picture cards that show both Level 1 Respect and Level 0 Disrespect in what I call a poster talk. These picture cards can be found on the CD (Level 1 Respect\Posters\Respect Poster Talk K-1). Make a vertical RESPECT sign that shows what each letter stands for: **r**ules, **e**quipment, **s**elf, **p**eople, **e**very **c**hild, and **t**eacher.

Make three strips of paper the same size as the vertical RESPECT sign; make one red, one green, and the third any color of your choice. Glue the vertical RESPECT letters on the third color of paper and laminate all three strips. Make two picture cards for each letter—one that shows Level 1 Respect (the happy picture) and one that shows Level 0 Disrespect (the sad picture)—and laminate.

Using hook-and-loop tape fasteners, place soft pieces of tape on the red and green strips of laminated paper and the rough pieces on the pictures. When you place the tape on the laminated paper, make sure to line up the tape and the pictures so they are even with each capital letter on the vertical RESPECT sign (see the illustration on page 39 for layout of signs).

level 1

respect

Following the rules of hide-and-seek.

From S. Hagenbach, 2011, *Teaching children responsible behavior: A complete toolkit* (Champaign, IL: Human Kinetics).

Happy picture card showing Level 1 Respect for K-1 respect poster talk.

Not following the rules of hide-and-seek.

From S. Hagenbach, 2011, *Teaching children responsible behavior: A complete toolkit* (Champaign, IL: Human Kinetics).

Sad picture card showing Level 0 for K-1 respect poster talk.

R Rules
Play fair
Follow the rules
Be honest

From S. Hagenbach, 2011, *Teaching children responsible behavior: A complete toolkit* (Champaign, IL: Human Kinetics).

Respect letters for K-1 respect poster talk.

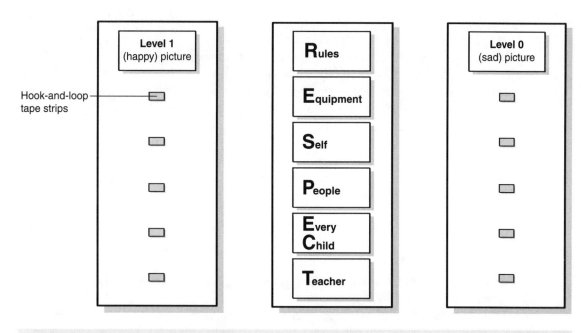

Layout of banners for the K-1 poster talk.

Post the three strips of paper next to each other with the word Respect in the middle of the green and red strip. Green is for the go behavior of respect and red is for the stop behavior of disrespect. I also put a smiley face above the green and a frown above the red paper. Have students sit down by the RESPECT sign and explain that Level 1 is respect. Next, show the two pictures for rules showing Level 1 Respect and Level 0 Disrespect. Give the pictures to two different children and let them put them on the correct green or red paper by lining up the hook-and-loop tape. Continue with the remaining pictures for each letter.

After the review, we practice Level 1 Respect for rules and talk about being honest by playing a simple game. I like to use the game Pigs Out of the Pen. Kindergarten students may not be ready for this game yet and may need to work first on moving safely in a general space. This is one of the first games I teach kindergarteners when my focus is following rules.

o PIGS OUT OF THE PEN

Equipment

- ▶ 1 or 2 large 36-inch beach balls or cage balls
- ▶ 3 or 4 smaller beach balls
- ▶ 1 playground ball per student
- ▶ 4 large cones to mark the corners of the square

Description

This is a throwing game for kindergarten through fourth grade students. Form a large square using floor lines with cones placed at the corners to mark the square. (Make the square larger for older students.) Place all of the small and large beach balls in the center of the square (pen). See the diagram on page 40. Divide class into four teams. Each team stands on one side of the square. Each student starts with a playground

level 1

respect

ball trapped at her feet. To challenge older students you may add more pigs or deflate some of the pigs a bit so the balls don't roll as quickly.

On the cue "Pigs out of the pen!" all the students throw playground balls at the beach balls in the center of the square. They are trying to get the beach balls to roll out of the square over another team's line. To stop a pig from going over a line the ball must be thrown, a student should not hold on to a ball and block the pig from going over the line. Besides respecting rules by being honest, the emphasis is on aiming. If you use smaller balls, the emphasis could change to using the correct form of overhand throw.

Designate an area to be the farm house. You can put up a picture of a farm house on the board or write the words *farm house* on the board to add some literacy. Students must sit out one game and go to the farm house if they break any of the following rules:

▶ If a pig bites a student (a beach ball touches him) he is out, and he must go to the farm house for a bandage.

▶ If a student steps into the square to retrieve a playground ball and gets all muddy, he must go to the farm house to take a bath. It is ok for students to get down on hands and knees to reach for a ball they can throw again, but they must keep their feet out of the square and in the grass, not the mud. It is a continous throwing game. Students pick up any loose ball and throw. According to the rules they may not touch a beach ball so the only ball to throw is a playground ball.

▶ Once a pig (beach ball) is out, do not hit it back into the square or the student has a time-out in the farm house for not respecting a pig.

▶ If a student kicks any ball, she must have a time out in the farm house.

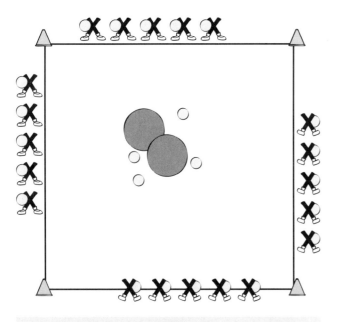

Setup for Pigs Out of the Pen.

When all the pigs are out of the pen, call, "Freeze!" to signal the game is over. Students should set up the game and get ready to play again. The teacher should always be in charge of the big pigs (balls). You may have the teams rotate to the left after each game. Games may last one to two minutes. Students should not sit out long. If the game is dragging, start giving a countdown at the end of which you call the end of the game.

Another way to practice Level 1 Respect for rules, or honesty, is to play the following game presented at a workshop by Jane Koval of Madison, Wisconsin. During a modified Four Square game, students practice serving and calling themselves out. If a student makes a mistake or misses the ball, she simply says, "Oops! I'm out," and the ball is given back to the server. After either three "oops" or three serves, students rotate, and a new server gets to practice. In this game students are simultaneously practicing Level 1 Respect for Rules, are playing at Level 2 Challenge as they practice skills, and hopefully are practicing Level 3 Teamwork, being a friendly during this game. Getting this game to add to my collection demonstrated for me the value of attending workshops. Workshops are a great way to connect, communicate, and collaborate with colleagues.

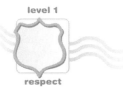

level 1

respect

○ RESPECT PUZZLE RELAY

Equipment

► RESPECT letter pieces to create puzzle pieces and banner (on the CD, Level 1 Respect\Activities\Respect Puzzle Relay). You will need one banner set of puzzle pieces for each team.

► Every Child questionnaire, one for each team (on the CD, Level 1 Respect\Activities\Respect Puzzle Relay).

Description

I use this activity to review Level 1 Respect with fourth grade students. To make puzzle pieces, copy the RESPT letter sheets from the CD. E and C are not used as puzzle pieces but are included in a questionnaire. The Every Child questionnaire will be the first piece of the puzzle used. Make enough puzzle sets for the number of groups you plan to have doing the activity. I use four squads and have four sets of puzzle pieces. Cut each letter sheet into three puzzle pieces: For example, the R sheet would be cut into pieces for the R, the word rules, and the demonstration showing respect of rules.

The letter sheets can also be used to make a banner that can be displayed as the students enter the gym. You can use one of these banners for a quick review of what Level 1 Respect looks like before the puzzle relay. This can give the students a guide for the relay or it can be a cheat sheet. Each group of students will create its own banner when the puzzle relay is over. I then pick

Respect Puzzle Banner pieces.

Every Child questionnaire.

up the puzzle pieces and scatter them for the next class. Make one copy of the Every Child questionnaire for each group.

Scatter all the puzzle pieces randomly in the middle of the gym. Have students get into groups, giving each group one Every Child questionnaire. The questionnaire sheet has a few "get to know you" questions. On the back of the questionnaire print the EC letters. This is the team's first puzzle piece. The group members must answer all the questions before they start the relay so they start making connections and get to know every child. Remind students that the E for every means including all children, no matter how they look, what their abilities are, what they own, how old they are, or if they are boys or girls. Students run out one at a time and pick up one puzzle piece until the RESPECT banner is put together. Thanks to Jackie Clark of Waupun, Wisconsin for the puzzle relay idea.

○ WARM-UP CHANT

Use this chant with a squat thrust or burpee:

Squat down, hands on ground: "R-E-S"
Jump feet back into a push-up position: "P-E-C-T"
Return to squat: "Respect, Respect."
Jump to a stand and clap: "That's for me!"

○ SCOOTER CITY

Equipment

- ▶ Cones and domes in a variety of sizes
- ▶ Folding mats
- ▶ Jump ropes
- ▶ Balls
- ▶ Fitness equipment of your choice
- ▶ Books, markers, and other reading and writing tools
- ▶ Rope and neckties
- ▶ Large box
- ▶ Small table and chairs
- ▶ Paper plates and paper cutouts of food pictures

Description

This activity is very popular with my students, and it's a great way to reinforce respect (especially for rules). I use Scooter City at the end of the year and set it up for a few days so students have a chance to go through the course at least twice. Scooter City allows students to play in an active, safe environment where they get to choose many of their activities. So often we forget to let kids be kids. I believe this activity is such a hit because students have the freedom to have so many choices while still being active and engaged in learning.

I create a city in the gym with streets, a gas station, a car wash, a drive-through bank, a jail, a health club, a restaurant, and a swimming pool. Students ride around on scooters to the various stations, some of which offer skill and fitness activities. While

level 1

respect

driving, they must follow traffic rules: stop at stop signs, drive on the correct side of the road, and so on. Students who break a rule are given a verbal ticket from the police officer. (You, the teacher, are the police officer—feel free to ride a scooter and make siren noises!) You can vary the tickets according to the severity of the infraction; for example, parking illegally might be a $10 ticket, whereas running a stop sign might be a $25 ticket. Students who are ticketed must go to jail, where they count to the number matching their ticket (for example, a student who got a $10 ticket would count to 10) and then may resume the activity.

Rules are as follows (infractions result in a ticket):

▶ While traveling on scooters, students' hands must remain in the guards.

▶ Students must travel on the right side of the road.

▶ Students must come to a complete stop at stop signs and look both ways before proceeding.

▶ When parking a scooter, students must turn it over.

▶ Students must pull over (turn over their scooter and stand up) if the police officer is traveling on their street with siren blaring.

▶ Students may not drive through any of the parks.

▶ Students should travel at a safe speed.

▶ Students should travel forward as if driving a car—no spinning donuts in the middle of a street.

▶ Students wishing to go to school must legally park their car in the school parking lot and then use the crosswalk to get to school. Students should only spend a short time in the school.

▶ At a school crossing, students using the crosswalk must look both ways and may not walk in the street.

▶ Cars should be parked in parking lots or between cones marking parks. No parking on city streets.

To set up the activity, mark off areas of the city as shown in the diagram on page 44. You can print the signs on the CD (Level 1 Respect\Activities\Scooter City) to post at the various stations. Streets are marked off within a basketball court. Many of the businesses are set up in the out-of-bounds area. (You may use cones, poly spots, tape, chalk, or any other marking equipment.) To create streets, I use domes and cones in a variety of sizes. To make the walls for the school and the one-way tunnel, I take folding mats and stand them on end accordion style. A roof can be added to the tunnel by using a smaller mat. I set up the basic course for the first day and add the school, restaurant, and bank on the second day. Some other instructions for setup are as follows:

▶ **Jump rope park:** Set out enough jump ropes for about 6 students to use. When arriving at the park, students park their scooters and jump rope.

▶ **Catching park:** Set out enough balls for 2 to 6 students to use. Students must look both ways if retrieving a ball from the street or a ticket is given.

▶ **Health club:** Set out whatever equipment is needed for fitness activities—for example, medicine balls and stretch bands. I have 6 activities and put one activity card on each side of a die. Students roll the die and do the activity. (The health club idea came from Kris Boggess, a fellow De Pere physical education teacher.)

level 1

respect

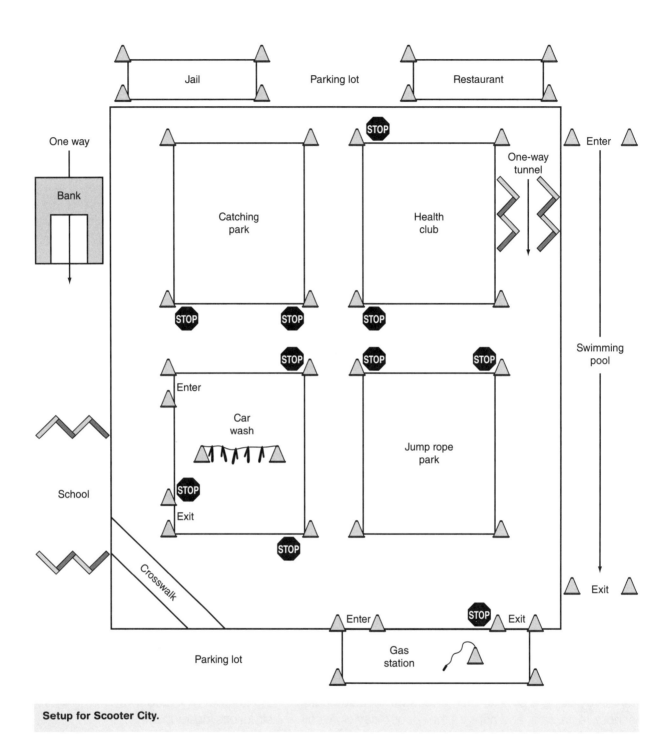

Setup for Scooter City.

▶ **Swimming pool:** Students scoot on their tummy. No diving onto scooters. Students should wait until the person in front of them is halfway through before starting into the pool. No swimming on city streets—swimming is allowed in the pool only!

▶ **Gas station:** Student must enter and exit at the correct spot. I have a play gas pump that students use. A modified version could be a jump rope (hose) hanging out of a cone (pump).

▶ **Car wash:** Suspend a rope between two large cones; hang neckties from the rope as the sweeping scrubbers. Students must enter and exit at the correct spot.

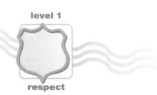

▶ **Bank:** You can use a large box (such as that used for a refrigerator) to represent the bank. Cut a door in the box. Students drive through and pretend to save money. They must merge into traffic safely.

▶ **School:** Set out school supplies such as books, worksheets, markers and marker board, and flash cards. Students may look at a book, do math on the board, or do a written activity. Students should spend only a short time at the school station.

▶ **School crosswalk:** Tape a crosswalk on the floor and connect the parking lot to the school (see setup on page 44).

▶ **Restaurant**: Set out a small table and a few chairs. Place a food guide pyramid poster on the table or on the wall. Place a few paper plates and a bowl of cut-out food images on the table. Students must place one healthy food from each food group on their plate before they leave the restaurant. If you see patrons in the restaurant, try to pass by to check on their food choices.

From S. Hagenbach, 2011, *Teaching children responsible behavior: A complete toolkit* (Champaign, IL: Human Kinetics).

Scooter City signs.

▶ **Parking lots**: Put a parking lot sign on the wall or on a cone to designate where students park their cars legally while at school or jail.

▶ **Bus**: If you have a large two-person scooter or scooters that hook together you can make a bus or two. I have three buses that I put out on the second day. Students sit back to back with the driver going forward and the passenger going backward. When using buses I stop and rotate students so everyone interested in riding a bus gets a chance. I also point out that Friendlies share and that students may ask a bus driver and passenger to switch at any time.

Reflecting on Level 1 Respect

At the end of class, we form two lines facing the word wall where our *I can* statements are displayed. *I can* statements are outcome driven and are posted in child-friendly language so students know what they are learning. We talk about what we have learned by reviewing our *I can* statements which is the focus of the lesson for the day. I have a pocket chart on the same wall that I use for informal assessment and reflection. At the top of the pocket chart, I have the letters R E S P E C T displayed. I also have little Respectaroo chips that I use to graph how students did with each of the components of respect. These can be found on the CD (Level 1 Respect\ Reflection\Graph). I or a student will place the chips in the pocket chart under the corresponding letter. For example, if students did an awesome job of freezing when asked, I may put a Respectaroo chip under the R, for respecting rules, or the T, for following directions. If students picked up equipment between station rotations, I may put a Respectaroo chip under the letter E, for respecting equipment. Students can see how they are using Level 1 Respect by looking at the graph.

level 1

respect

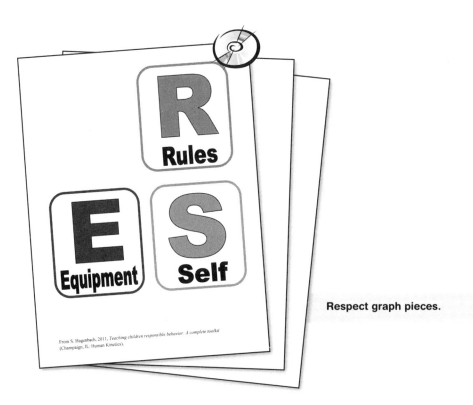

Respect graph pieces.

From S. Hagenbach, 2011, *Teaching children responsible behavior: A complete toolkit* (Champaign, IL: Human Kinetics).

From S. Hagenbach, 2011, *Teaching children responsible behavior: A complete toolkit* (Champaign, IL: Human Kinetics).

Level touch chart.

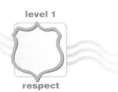

You can also use the thumbs-up assessment at the end of class to allow students to think about where they were during class. Thumbs-up means they showed Level 1 Respect most of the time during class, thumbs-to-the-side means they showed respect some of the time, and thumbs-down means they need to try harder at working at Level 1. Students may also touch a level poster on the way out of the gym to show what levels they were working at during class. There are two level posters on the CD that could be displayed. These are in the All Levels folder.

The homework activities included on the CD (Level 1 Respect\Reflection\Homework and Assessments) can serve a variety of purposes, including reflection. They may be used by classroom teachers who incorporate the levels into the classroom or have the responsibility of teaching physical education. Physical education teachers can use them on days when they are asked to give up their teaching space for special events, or they may use them as assessments. They may also be used to reinforce the concepts taught in class as physical education homework.

There are six homework activities to reinforce Level 1 Respect. For primary students, homework is either drawing a picture of being a Respectaroo or drawing lines from the Respectaroo to the picture that demonstrates respect. These could be used as formal assessments. A special Words of Wisdom activity has students fill in the blank with letters from the word Respect to answer two questions. This would be appropriate for first or second grade students. There is also a word search activity (a key is included) and crossword puzzle along with a reflective piece that asks upper level (grades 3 and 4) students how they can show respect at home, in the classroom, and in the community. The crossword puzzle could serve as an assessment also. The reflective homework that asks how the student can apply level 1 outside of physical education can be another great assessment.

The CD also includes a reader for students in third or fourth grade (Level 1 Respect\Reflection\Reader). This activity places what students have learned about Level 1 Respect into real life situations. The physical education teacher could use this as a rainy day activity or as homework, with a discussion to follow during the next class. When I give homework, which is not often, the homework is due at the beginning of class. All who have it done immediately get to play a game. Those who do not have it completed must finish the work before they join the activity. I explain my expectations when I hand out the homework so students are aware of what will happen if the homework is not completed. Remember, if you have connected with classroom teachers, they may collaborate with you and do the weekly reader activity in the classroom for you.

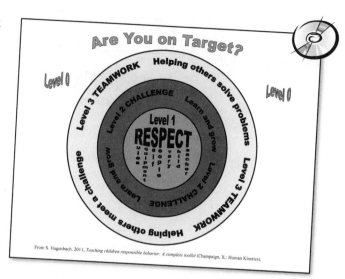

Level touch target poster.

Once all three levels have been introduced and practiced, students may periodically fill out a How Are You Doing assessment. There is a simple one that students fill in with a smile, straight face, or frown. There is an advanced one that asks students to look at outcomes from the national standards and check where they've had success. Both assessments are included in the All Levels folder on the CD.

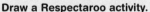

Draw a Respectaroo activity.

Matching activity.

RESPECTAROO
Words of Wisdom

Put the correct letter from RESPECT in the box by each picture.

Rules Equipment Self People Every Child Teacher

What words of wisdom are given to you?

To be a Respectaroo, you need to do your best in this class:

☐ ☐

To keep yourself healthy, you need to get plenty of this each night:

☐ ☐ ☐ ☐

Words of Wisdom activity.

RESPECTAROO

Find the words in the word search that describe what Respectaroos respect in physical education or what they do to show respect.

every child	no wild	people	friend
self	active	safe	respect
rules	honesty	equipment	put it away
respectaroo			

R	S	R	Y	I	K	G	N	B	D	T	U	R	U	F
E	Q	U	I	P	M	E	N	T	S	W	R	E	Y	R
S	A	T	M	U	B	G	M	O	D	M	I	S	G	I
P	C	A	C	T	I	V	E	K	P	E	O	P	L	E
E	W	T	U	I	V	O	B	J	L	N	T	E	U	N
C	W	E	T	T	Y	U	I	S	A	F	E	C	P	D
T	A	S	F	A	E	T	S	E	G	H	J	T	L	M
Z	X	C	V	W	B	N	M	L	L	K	J	A	G	F
D	S	A	Q	A	W	R	N	F	T	Y	U	R	I	O
P	P	L	K	Y	J	H	O	G	G	D	S	O	A	E
B	N	T	Y	O	P	G	W	N	D	O	R	O	D	N
E	V	E	R	Y	C	H	I	L	D	F	U	N	L	L
W	B	M	N	R	I	E	L	I	W	U	L	O	B	W
Z	X	C	N	M	P	S	D	H	O	N	E	S	T	Y
W	M	B	R	P	G	K	S	R	J	K	S	W	Y	I

Word Search activity.

RESPECTAROO

Word search answer key:

every child	no wild	people	friend
self	active	safe	respect
rules	honesty	equipment	put it away
respectaroo			

R	S	R	Y	I	K	G	N	B	D	T	U	R	U	F
E	Q	U	I	P	M	E	N	T	S	W	R	E	Y	R
S	A	T	M	U	B	G	M	O	D	M	I	S	G	I
P	C	A	C	T	I	V	E	K	P	E	O	P	L	E
E	W	T	U	I	V	O	B	J	L	N	T	E	U	N
C	W	E	T	T	Y	U	I	S	A	F	E	C	P	D
T	A	S	F	A	E	T	S	E	G	H	J	T	L	M
Z	X	C	V	W	B	N	M	L	L	K	J	A	G	F
D	S	A	Q	A	W	R	N	F	T	Y	U	R	I	O
P	P	L	K	Y	J	H	O	G	G	D	S	O	A	E
B	N	T	Y	O	P	G	W	N	D	O	R	O	D	N
E	V	E	R	Y	C	H	I	L	D	F	U	N	L	L
W	B	M	N	R	I	E	L	I	W	U	L	O	B	W
Z	X	C	N	M	P	S	D	H	O	N	E	S	T	Y
W	M	B	R	P	G	K	S	R	J	K	S	W	Y	I

Key for Word Search activity.

Level 1 RESPECT

Rules Equipment Self People Every Child Teacher

Fill in the crossword puzzle with the correct words.

every child	equipment	people	respect
your	rules	teacher	self
school	parents		

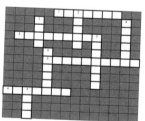

Across
1. At home your ____ are your teachers.
2. Take care of it, do not play when you put it away, show respect to ____.
3. Don't go wild, keep them safe, show respect to ____.
4. What you should show in physical education.

Down
1. It is ____ choice to be at Level 1 Respect.
2. The key is honesty is to show respect to ____.
3. Two eyes watching, two ears listening, and one mouth quiet all show respect to the ____.
4. Be a friend—show respect to ____.
5. Be active and be safe—show respect to ____.
6. Show respect at home and in ____.

Crossword activity.

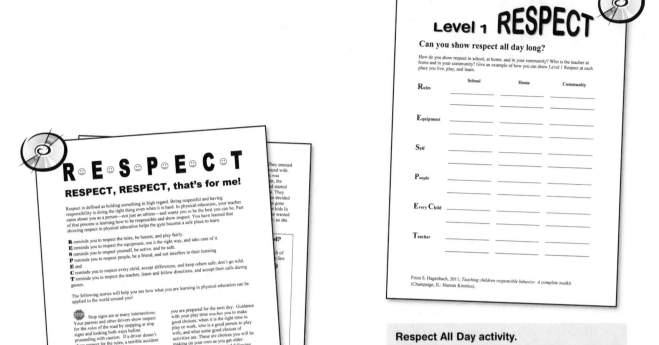

Respect All Day activity.

Respect reader.

How Are You Doing assessment for kindergarten through second grade.

How Are You Doing?

Student _____ Teacher _____

Put a + in the box if the statement is something you do most of the time in physical education.
Put a √ in the box if the statement is something you do sometimes in physical education.
Put a – in the box if the statement is something you could improve on in physical education.

Level 1 Respect	Level 2 Challenge	Level 3 Teamwork
☐ I use honesty to follow rules.	☐ I practice, practice, practice until my teacher signals the end.	☐ I try not to argue and I use acceptable conflict resolution during class.
☐ I use equipment the right way and take care of it.	☐ I work independently and think, think, think while practicing.	☐ I regularly encourage others and I don't use put-downs.
☐ I keep myself and others safe.	☐ I challenge myself without my teacher's reminders.	☐ I cooperate with ALL class members by taking turns and sharing equipment.
☐ I show respect for people and every child by being kind, taking turns, sharing, and not interfering.	☐ I try new skills and movements willingly.	☐ I am a friend to **all**.
☐ I listen attentively to my teacher and follow directions.	☐ I participate even when I'm not successful.	☐ I help others solve problems or meet challenges.
☐ I take responsibility for my own behavior.		

If you marked any box with a √ or –, how can you improve your choices?

What is the level you work at the best? Why?

From S. Hagenbach, 2011, *Teaching children responsible behavior: A complete toolkit* (Champaign, IL: Human Kinetics).

How Are You Doing assessment for grades three and four.

Communicating With Parents

Getting parents involved is an important part of any physical education program. Parents need to know your expectations just as your students do. At the elementary level especially, the parents want to know what their children are learning. This communication is a great way to affirm the integral part physical education plays in the development of the whole child.

The CD includes two letters you can send to parents for this unit: one explaining the three levels (in the All Levels folder), and another discussing the Respectaroo story (Level 1 Respect\Communication). The Respectaroo letter also includes a pledge sheet for the student to sign (when preparing the letter and pledge to send home to parents, you can use one piece of paper, placing the letter on the front and the pledge on the back). There is power in choice, and with it comes the feeling of satisfaction for doing the right things. This pledge sheet gives the student the power to choose to be a Respectaroo. The reward for doing well is the satisfaction of being a Respectaroo.

Another communication tool is the Elementary Physical Education Progress Report based on the NASPE national standards and outcomes found in the book *Moving into the future: National standards for physical education* (2004). Teachers may use either the *concern* report or the *excelling* report to inform parents of their child's progress between grading periods. This will help avoid surprising parents at grading periods. Both of these letters may be found in the All Levels folder on the CD.

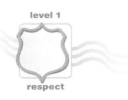

level 1

respect

Parent note explaining the Respectaroo story and student pledge.

Parent note explaining the three levels.

Progress report for students who are doing well.

Elementary Physical Education Progress Report

Student _____ Teacher _____

This note is to inform you of your child's progress toward meeting the following two national physical education standards:

- Exhibits responsible personal and social behavior that respects self and others in physical activity settings
- Values activity for health, enjoyment, challenge, self-expression, and social interaction

Below are three lists of outcomes, each representing a level of behavior expected in physical education. Checked are the areas of concern. **We would like to see your child improve in these areas.** Please talk with your child about these behavioral choices in physical education. I am hopeful we can work together to improve your child's choices before the next grading period. If you have any questions, please feel free to call or email me.

Level 1 Respect	Level 2 Challenge	Level 3 Teamwork
☐ Follows rules, directions, procedures, and etiquette in class	☐ Practices assigned skills until the teacher signals the end	☐ Demonstrates the elements of socially acceptable conflict resolution during class activity
☐ Uses safety procedures	☐ Works independently and productively	☐ Regularly encourages others and refrains from put-down statements
☐ Works in a diverse group setting without interfering with others	☐ Demonstrates a willingness to challenge self	☐ Shows cooperation and fair play for others by helping, sharing, and taking turns
☐ Listens attentively during directions	☐ Attempts new movements and skills willingly	☐ Accepts all peers without regard to personal differences
☐ Takes responsibility for his or her own behavior	☐ Participates even when not successful	☐ Shares and takes turns
☐ Accepts teacher's decision without a negative response		
☐ Demonstrates safe control of body and equipment		

Comments:

From S. Hagenbach, 2011, *Teaching children responsible behavior: A complete toolkit* (Champaign, IL: Human Kinetics).

Progress report for students who need improvement.

Supporting Standards and Performance Outcomes

All of our activities and lesson designs should support our standards, benchmarks, and outcomes. Level 1 Respect addresses NASPE National Standard 5: Exhibits responsible personal and social behavior that respects self and others in physical activity settings (2004). Some performance outcomes (NASPE 2004, unless otherwise noted) are listed here as examples of those that relate to respect.

With each sample outcome, I have also included some corresponding child-friendly learning targets written as *I can* statements that refer to respect in terms of the standards and outcomes. The push in our district, as it is in education nationally, is to provide students with learning targets, in the belief that students learn more if they know what they are expected to learn. These targets should be written in child-friendly language and should be posted in the classroom. Teachers should address these targets at some time in their lessons. We strive to post our learning targets in every subject: math, reading, physical education, art, music, social studies, and science.

Practices specific skill as assigned until the teacher signals the end of practice.
  – *I can challenge myself when practicing in PE and freeze when asked.*

Follows directions given to the class for an all-class activity.
  – *I can follow directions in PE.*

Handles equipment safely and uses it appropriately.
  – *I can take care of my equipment and use it safely.*

Attentively listens to teacher during instruction (Unified School District of DePere/Tribes Agreement, Gibbs 2001)
  – *I can show respect to the teacher and be a good listener during directions.*

Accepts all playmates without regard to personal differences.
  – *I can play with all of my classmates with respect.*

Participates safely in class activities.
  – *I can stay safe in PE.*

Honestly reports the results of work or rule infractions.
  – *I can be honest during games and practice time.*

Accepts teacher's decision without a negative response.
  – *I can follow the decision of a teacher on the rules and not argue during a game.*

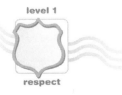

level 1

respect

Summary

Level 1 Respect is the foundation of the three modified elementary levels. Students showing respect toward rules, equipment, and others will make your classroom a safe place both physically and emotionally where all students can learn. Without Level 1 Respect your students will not be able to challenge themselves at Level 2 Challenge or participate at Level 3 Teamwork. If you choose to concentrate your efforts on any one of the levels, start here.

Who Wears Gym Shoes?

A Respectaroo!

Sandy Hagenbach

Respect
Rules

Respect the RULES is what you should do
if you want to be a Respectaroo!

Rules
Equipment
Self
People
Every
Child
Teacher

Rules make games fun, safe, and fair.
So follow them to show that you care.

Honesty is the key to following rules.
Make it one of your everyday tools!

r**E**spect
Equipment

Respect the EQUIPMENT is what you should do
if you want to be a Respectaroo!

Rules
Equipment
Self
People
Every
Child
Teacher

Equipment can break, and that would be sad.
So be responsible, please, and make everyone glad!

Rules
Equipment
Self
People
Every
Child
Teacher

Please don't play as you put things away.
Just do your job the Respectaroo way!

re**S**pect
elf

Respect your SELF is what you should do
if you want to be a Respectaroo!

Rules
Equipment
Self
People
Every
Child
Teacher

You have to choose to make your heart strong,
so get it pumping and keep moving along!

Rules
Equipment
Self
People
Every
Child
Teacher

As you move around in general space,
be careful to stay in your own safe place.

res**P**ect
People

Respect other PEOPLE is what you should do
if you want to be a Respectaroo!

Rules
Equipment
Self
People
Every
Child
Teacher

People come in all colors, shapes, and sizes.
Being a friend to all is one of life's prizes!

Protect people's feelings is what you should do.
Be a praise-giving friend—be a Respectaroo!

respECt
very hild

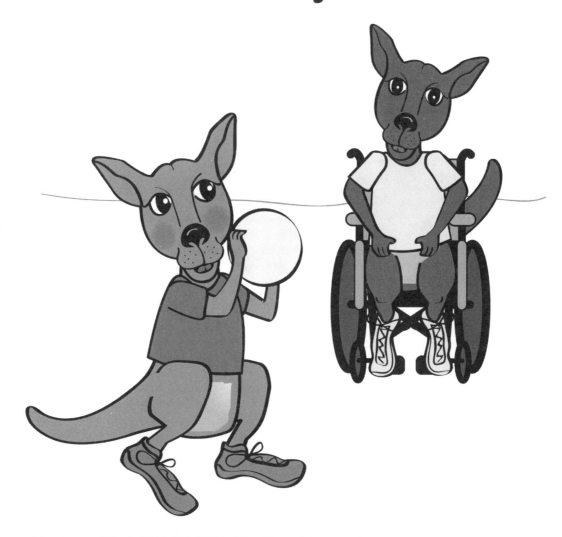

Respect **EVERY CHILD** is what you should do
if you want to be a Respectaroo!

Rules
Equipment
Self
People
Every
Child
Teacher

Respecting PEOPLE includes EVERY CHILD.
Keep them safe. Stay calm. Don't go wild!

Respect the TEACHER is what you should do
if you want to be a Respectaroo!

Your quiet mouth, listening ears, and watching eyes will show your teacher that you are wise.

When you follow directions, you'll be safe and grow.
Your teacher wants to help you more than you know!

R**ules**
Equipment
Self
People
Every
Child
Teacher

In physical education what should you do?
Always try to be a responsible Respectaroo!

Follow the rules
and be honest

• • • • • •

Take care of it

• • • • • •

Be safe and active

• • • • •

Be a friend

• • • • • • •

Don't go wild

• • • • • • •

Listen to and
follow directions

• • • • •

Challenge

As teachers, we try each day to guide and motivate our students while providing well-designed lessons with developmentally appropriate progressions. But ultimately, our students choose whether to learn, so we also need to teach them how to challenge themselves. Then they will have the chance to reach their potential.

Here is the mission statement at my school, Heritage Elementary in De Pere, Wisconsin: "Every person, every day, will learn grow and help others to feel respected and valued." This mission statement has helped me define my teaching and has validated the three levels used in my classes. Teachers pride themselves in providing a challenging curriculum and activities, but unless we provide an environment where students are free to challenge themselves and understand how to go about it, we are falling short of our goal: every student learning and growing every day.

Children's Story

The illustrated children's story "Where Will You Be After PE?" (page 101; also on the CD in Level 2 Challenge\Story) helps teach both why and how a student should become a Challenger. The story has two main characters. Challengers, the superheroes of the story, make choices that improve their skills through hard work. (They are represented as both boys and girls from different cultures with a variety of abilities.) Wasters squander time and do not reach their potential. (They are illustrated as stick figures to avoid attaching negative connotations to any element of appearance.) As the story evolves, the Wasters figure out they want to become Challengers and morph over time. As you read the story, point out how the Waster is changing. Remind students they can choose to be Challengers.

Students learn that to reach their potential, to learn and grow, they must work hard and challenge themselves. The story gives examples of children challenging themselves as they develop physical skills by changing direction, adding more repetitions, adding distance, changing the side of the body emphasized, and pushing their limits. Students will learn why and how to challenge themselves; they also learn that they have a choice, that they can choose to change and to make good choices to

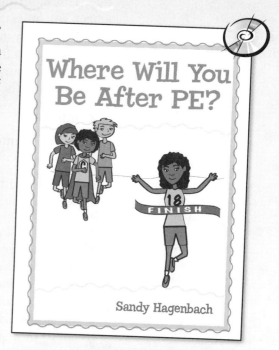

"Where Will You Be After PE?" is on page 101 and the CD.

reach their potential. This story is great for the beginning of second grade to introduce or reinforce the concept of challenging oneself or working at Level 2 Challenge. It can be used with first graders at the beginning of the year or as a review midyear.

This is also consistent with the goals of many community programs. The refrains "Taking responsibility for our choices is what we need, to be Challengers who most certainly will succeed" and "Being responsible is right for me; there is no stopping what I can be!" reinforce the YMCA core value of responsibility.

Introducing Level 2 Challenge

When introducing the challenge level, it's important to emphasize that students need to be at Level 1 Respect so the class is safe, and the gym can be a place where everyone can learn. If they want to learn, Level 2 Challenge is the level they need to reach. Keep in mind that the levels are interconnected. Most students who participate at Level 2 Challenge will also be at Level 1 Respect. Have your students live the levels every day. Be constantly consistent by reinforcing the levels throughout all of your lessons.

Being consistent with the language or terms you use is important when addressing behaviors. The story "Where Will You Be After PE?" will give you some of that language: Being a Challenger will get you to where you want to go. Being a Waster is a waste of time. Time is something we can never get back, so it needs to be used wisely.

This is the way I describe a challenge: A challenge is not easy. You must think and work hard. In doing this, you will get better at something old or learn something new. This description can be simplified for younger children: When you are a challenger, you must think, think, think, and practice, practice, practice. I also tell them, "If it is too easy, make it a challenge." Posters showing both of these descriptions are included on the CD (Level 2 Challenge\Posters).

There are four characteristics of a good challenge that students will need to understand as they develop into Challengers.

1. It is safe.
2. It doesn't interfere with others' activities.
3. It is added to a skill you do well, or it is a new skill.
4. It is met with practice, not luck.

A poster showing these characteristics is included on the CD (Level 2 Challenge\Posters).

There are several techniques that can be used to create a challenge. Most involve changing something or adding something to the activity once it is mastered. A student could change different components of the basic action: distance, speed, height, target, direction, side of body, or equipment. Another option is to add a trick, an additional movement, focus points to form, more tries, additional people, more kinds or a greater amount of equipment, or an additional skill. As challengers, students will be personalizing their own skill practices.

Once the concept of Level 2 Challenge has been introduced, you will need to provide a variety of challenges and the opportunity for students to create their own.

level 2

challenge

Poster with description of a challenge for third and fourth grades.

Poster with description of a challenge for kindergarten to second grade.

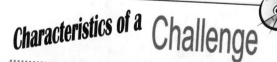

Poster showing characteristics of a challenge.

Catch students at Level 2 Challenge. Positive reinforcement is the way to go. If a student is off task, simply ask if she is being a challenger; is she working at Level 2 Challenge? Don't ask if she is being a waster. Use positive language when possible.

The I Spy, I Try poster (on the CD, Level 2 Challenge\Posters) is an introduction to Level 2 Challenge for kindergarteners and can be a review for first graders. As they are searching the Waldo-like poster for the students at Level 2 Challenge, use the term *challenger* as they spy the students hard at work. Remember that this common language helps students remember. This common language also makes your expectations clear and understandable.

I use the story "Where Will You Be After PE?" with first and second grade. Staying on task and working hard are the focus for first grade, while creating challenges is an additional focus for second grade. If you chose to use the I Spy, I Try poster talk to introduce Level 2 Challenge at the beginning of the year with first graders, use this story as a review in the middle of the year when students need a quick refresher on Level 2 Challenge. The posters that reinforce the key characteristics of challenges and the methods of creating challenges are used with third and fourth graders. These are on the CD in the Posters folder for Level 2. You know your students and program; use the resources to fit them and their abilities.

From S. Hagenbach, 2011, *Teaching children responsible behavior: A complete toolkit* (Champaign, IL: Human Kinetics).

I Spy, I Try poster.

Creating Challenges

Change
Distance
Speed
Height
Target
Direction
Side of body
Equipment

Add
A trick
Movement
Checkpoints to form
Number of tries
More people
Equipment
Another skill

Create a new challenge only if you have mastered the challenge given by your teacher.

From S. Hagenbach, 2011, *Teaching children responsible behavior: A complete toolkit* (Champaign, IL: Human Kinetics).

Poster showing ways to create a challenge.

level 2

challenge

After students have spied the *I Tries* in the I Spy, I Try poster, we play a throwing game and work on becoming Challengers by working at Level 2 Challenge. Splash and Spiders in the Web are the same game but with equipment modifications to make the games easier for kindergarten or more challenging for the first grade.

o SPLASH

Equipment

▶ 1 beanbag or Beanie Baby per student

▶ 7 to 10 blue hula hoops, preferably of different sizes

▶ Music to stop and start game

Description

Scatter the hoops on the floor. Give each student a beanbag or Beanie Baby (I use Mickey and Minnie Mouse Beanie Babies) and have students spread out in the room. Before giving directions, you may want to remind students to work at Level 1 Respect: Follow the rules and be honest. Keep building your culture.

When the music is played, students walk around, tossing the beanbags and then catching them themselves. When the music stops, students catch their beanbags and freeze in place. On your signal "Splash," students choose a hoop that will be a challenge for them (distance or size) and throw the beanbag towards the selected hoop. A point is scored if the beanbag splashes in the hoop (stays in, bounces in, or lands in and bounces out). Students wait to pick up their beanbag until the music starts again. When they first play the game, remind students, before the signal to throw, what a challenge is and how they can become Challengers. Later in the year I will play this game focusing on the form of the throw.

o SPIDERS IN THE WEB

Equipment

▶ 1 Spider Ball per student

▶ 6 to 8 laundry baskets (I got mine from the dollar store)

▶ Music to stop and start game

Description

Scatter baskets on the floor. Give each student a Spider Ball and have them spread out in general space. Before giving directions, you may want to remind students to work at Level 1 Respect: Follow the rules, be honest, and show respect towards the equipment. Keep building your culture.

When the music starts playing, students walk around, tossing and catching their Spider Balls. When the music stops, students catch their Spider Balls and freeze in place. On your signal "Spiders in the web," students choose a basket that will be a challenge for them to throw at. Two points are scored if the ball lands in the *web* (the laundry basket), and one point is scored if the ball hits the web. Students wait to pick up their ball until the music starts again. When they first play the game, remind students, before each signal of "Spiders in the web," what a challenge is and how they can become challengers. Students could also make up challenges on the self-tossing and catching by adding a clap or a trick or changing the height to the toss. A bounce and catch could be another alternative to the toss and catch.

level 2

challenge

Reinforcing Level 2 Challenge

Letting students create their own challenges is a great way to teach and reinforce the concept of Level 2 Challenge, and it allows the student to collaborate with you. You can create a variety of stations with a different challenge at each. Students are asked to meet your challenge and then create their own. I use this activity with students in third and fourth grade at the beginning of the year as an introduction or review of Level 2 Challenge.

○ CHALLENGE STATIONS

Equipment

- ▶ A tub of 4 or 5 basketballs and two large cones
- ▶ Another tub of 8 to 10 basketballs
- ▶ 4 to 6 jump ropes
- ▶ 4 or 5 rackets with the same number of small and large balls to hit
- ▶ 4 or 5 wall posters or boards that have both small and large targets with balls to throw
- ▶ 4 to 6 scoops and a variety of balls to catch
- ▶ 4 to 6 Koosh balls and 4 to 6 poly spots

Description

Before the station activity, review the challenge posters on the CD (in the Posters folder for Level 2) with the class: the description of a challenge, characteristics of a good challenge, and creating challenges. Remind them that good challenges are safe and non-interfering and are added to skills already acquired. They are also expected to think about their form when working on challenges. Thinking about form is vital and should be emphasized. The brain still needs to be working even if the body is doing the learning.

Set up stations using the Challenge Cards included on the CD (Level 2 Challenge\Activities\Challenge Stations). There is an easy Challenge Card for second grade and a harder Challenge Card for third and fourth graders. The cards can be copied and glued to a file folder. Glue the easy card on the inside of the file folder and the harder challenge on the outside. Cut a hole in the middle of the file folder so it will fit over a cone. Laminate the folders. You can easily switch between easy and more difficult challenges simply by flipping the file folder over.

STATION 1

Have enough basketballs so each student has the option of dribbling two balls at once.

Easy: Dribble a basketball in your favorite hand 10 times.

Hard: Dribble a basketball in your favorite hand 25 times.

Student challenge ideas: Students may increase the number of tries, change the hand they use, add a trick, add equipment (a second ball), or add movement.

STATION 2

Have two differently sized fluff balls for the easy challenge and add one or two more types of balls for the harder challenge.

level 2

challenge

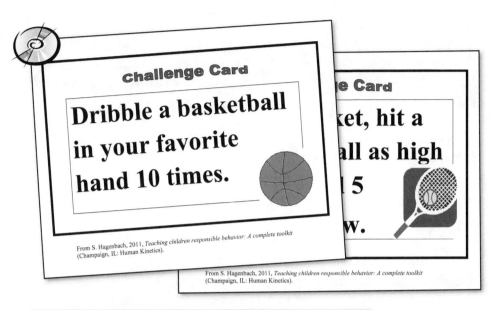

Challenge Card

Dribble a basketball in your favorite hand 10 times.

From S. Hagenbach, 2011, *Teaching children responsible behavior: A complete toolkit* (Champaign, IL: Human Kinetics).

...e Card

...ket, hit a ...all as high ...l 5 ...w.

From S. Hagenbach, 2011, *Teaching children responsible behavior: A complete toolkit* (Champaign, IL: Human Kinetics).

Challenge Cards for Challenge Stations activity.

Easy: With a racket, hit a large fluff ball as high as your head 5 times in a row.

Hard: With a racket, hit a ball as high as your head 10 times in a row.

Student challenge ideas: Students may increase the number of tries, change the height the ball rises, change the size or type of ball, add movement (forehand/ backhand), add people and hit to each other.

STATION 3

Set up a poster or board that has both a large and small target. I painted targets on a solid colorful piece of material using a 36-inch hula hoop as a guide for the large target and an Olympet 20-inch ring for the small target. Since I use these targets when I assess my throws, I use standard size targets. The cloth targets are easy to tape up and take down. Have two lines for students to stand behind: one for the easy challenge and one a little farther back for the harder challenge.

Easy: Concentrating on using good form, students try to hit a large target with an overhand throw 3 out of 5 times.

Hard: Concentrating on using good form, students try to hit a large target with an overhand throw 7 out of 10 times.

Student challenge ideas: Students can increase the number of tries, aim for the smaller target, add speed, back up to increase the distance, or add more check- points for the form of the throw.

STATION 4

Have a variety of differently sized jump ropes available to students.

Easy: Turn the rope forward and jump 10 times without missing.

Hard: Turn the rope forward and jump 20 times without missing.

Student challenge ideas: Students may increase the number of tries, reverse the rope turn direction, change speed, add a trick, or add people.

level 2

challenge

STATION 5

Place two large cones at a distance apart so students can run a lap around them; supply a basketball for each student.

Easy: Dribble from one cone to the other and back using your favorite hand.

Hard: While jogging, dribble from one cone to the other and back using your favorite hand.

Student challenge ideas: Students may change side of body, add speed, add a trick, weave, or change direction.

STATION 6

Have enough scoops, balls that bounce, and balls that don't bounce for each student.

Easy: Catch a ball in a scoop 5 times in a row (whether or not it may bounce first is left up to the student).

Hard: Catch a ball in a scoop 10 times with no bounce.

Student challenge ideas: Students may increase the number of tries, change the ball used, change height of toss, add people, or change sides of body.

STATION 7

Put out a few poly spots to mark an easy distance apart for two partners to play catch. Feel free to increase the distance between spots for the harder challenge. Have a variety of balls to catch. One of the balls I use is a homemade foxtail-style or comet ball. I tie an old nylon scarf over a tennis ball. If a student misses catching the ball, he will often be successful at catching the tail.

Easy: Partners stand on the spots and catch a ball 5 times without dropping it.

Hard: Partners stand on the spots and catch a ball 10 times without dropping it.

Student challenge ideas: Students may increase the number of tries, increase the distance, change equipment, add movement, add equipment, or add people (such as a guard).

You may use all of the Challenge Cards, in which case time at each station will be short. Since you should leave time at the end of class for students to demonstrate their challenges and discuss how they were developed, students will not get to all seven stations in a thirty minute class period. Instead, you could select four or five cards and give the students more time at each station or let students choose stations. Either way, make sure there is time for students to demonstrate their challenges.

This lesson could also be done over two days. Set up all seven stations. Review the posters and then allow ample time for students to explore half of the stations, creating challenges for themselves. The next class, have students create challenges at the stations they missed. Let students demonstrate challenges and spend more time discussing the creation process. Remember to make the lesson your own.

o GOAL DAY

At the beginning of the year, I introduce the second grade to the concept of creating goals, and I tie the lesson into the concept of being a Challenger. It takes a few days to get Goal Day set up, but once it's done, we do Goal Day once a month through the school year. Goal Day has a soccer theme, and students try to score as many goals as possible.

Equipment

- ▶ 3 or 4 individual jump ropes
- ▶ 1 or 2 long jump ropes
- ▶ Poly spots
- ▶ 2 or 3 Koosh balls
- ▶ 4 or 5 basketballs
- ▶ 2 or 3 posters or boards that have both a large and small target and balls for throwing
- ▶ 2 or 3 rackets
- ▶ 2 or 3 large fluff balls to hit

Description

Set up eight goal stations to correspond to the goals listed on the goal sheet (on the CD, Level 2 Challenge\Activities\Goal Day). Over two days, let students get a baseline score for each skill. I use skills that students will be working on throughout the year or will be working on next year; you can customize the goal sheet to cover the skills that you're working on in your class. With the exception of dribbling, a partner must count the number of successful tries at every station. Students may count their own dribbling. Record the scores under the "I can" statements on the students' goal sheets.

The next time you discuss Goal Day, explain the difference between a realistic challenge goal and one that is unrealistic. I tell my students if the score is small, add a small number. If the score is large, add a large number. For example if a student can dribble 367 times, then adding 30 to 50 is a realistic challenge for a goal. If a student can hit a ball three times in a row with a racket, then adding 2 or 3 hits is a realistic challenge. Have students fill out the "I want to" statements with realistic challenging goals.

As students complete goals during monthly Goal Days, they come to me with their partners, who confirm that the goal has been met. I circle the goal and quickly write out two goal *Score* awards. One award is for the student to take home, and one is for the student to glue on the "Second Graders Are Scoring Goals" bulletin board. (Awards are on the CD, Level 2 Challenge\Activities\Goal Day.) This takes a little more time and organization. Choose what will work for you; when you do this for the first time, you might make just one award to either post on the bulletin board or send home. The following are the skills on the goal sheet: Shoot a basket 5 times, dribble a ball with your nonfavorite hand, do push-ups, hit a ball with a racket, throw to a large target, jump using a short rope, jump using a long rope, and play catch with a partner.

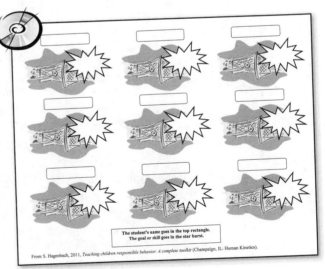

Goal sheet to be used in Goal Day activity.

Goal score awards for Goal Day activity.

level 2

challenge

○ FITNESS GOAL GRAPH

Level 2 Challenge is reinforced with fourth graders in conjunction with their fitness testing when they evaluate their test scores and then write a personal fitness goal. Once fitness testing is done, I have students graph their fitness scores using a spreadsheet (on the CD, Level 2 Challenge\Activities\Fitness Goal Graph). Students can easily tell which of their fitness scores indicate their strengths and which show their weaknesses through the graphing activity.

The graphs are based on five commonly used Fitnessgram fitness tests: PACER, curls, push-ups, arm hang, and sit-and-reach. These graphs show the Fitnessgram Healthy Fitness Zone (HFZ) for four of the tests for boys and girls ages 9-11. The fifth test, the PACER, does not indicate a Healthy Fitness Zone because results of the PACER are now reported as aerobic capacity ($\dot{V}O_2$max), which is based on each individual's height and weight. Instead, suggested levels for goal setting are shaded on the PACER graph so students can set goals by laps or levels.

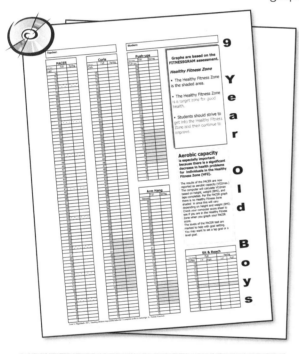

Fitness goal graphs.

Goal setting is a process. This may be one of your students' first attempts at setting, writing, working toward, and achieving their goal. Make it a successful one by helping them make realistic goals based on their body type. Remind students of the importance of maintaining a healthy weight or BMI; running more laps in the PACER test while increasing BMI could mean no improvement in one's PACER score.

Once a student has determined which test is her weakest, she then writes a fitness goal using a Fitness Goal Sheet (on the CD, Level 2 Challenge\Activities\Fitness Goal Graph). Remind students that reaching their goal is not guaranteed. They need to put in the time and have the motivation to succeed. I make an overhead copy of a blank goal sheet and project it onto the marker board, then go through the sheet and fill out a sample goal.

Help students understand what a realistic goal is. Body type and health issues can affect their performance and should be reflected in their goal setting. Once the students have completed their own goal sheets, they are copied. One copy is put in their fitness folders, and the original is sent home with their fitness scores, the graph, and a letter home explaining fitness testing.

Students will need help reaching their fitness goals. Post a list of students and their goals in the gym. This list should contain first names and the fitness test they are trying to improve: no scores are posted. Any time you call "Goal" and raise your arms, students work on their fitness goals. This could happen during skill practice or a game; everything stops, and students challenge themselves to improve their personal fitness. When you call "Goal," students working on flexibility and strength move to the inside, and those working on aerobics move to the outside. Here are some examples. Students doing

- ▶ aerobics run laps;
- ▶ curls may choose to do curls, knee bumps, bicycles, or V-sits;

▶ knee bumps lie in a curled position with their hands by their heads and, lifting their chests and knees, bump opposite elbow to knee, continuing to alternate opposite elbow to knee;

▶ arm hangs or push-ups may choose to do shoulder touches, over and backs, inchworms, or push-ups;

shoulder touches assume a push-up position and touch the shoulder with the opposite hand and continue by alternating shoulders and hands;

over and backs start in a push-up position with their hands behind a line and move their hands one at a time over the line and then back;

inchworms start in a push-up position and walk feet to hands, trying to keep their legs as straight as possible, and then walk their hands back into a push-up position;

▶ sit-and-reach do 20 seconds on each leg in a #4 stretch, a straddle stretch, or a hamstring stretch.

○ JUMP ROPE SKILL CHALLENGE

Good teachers develop learning experiences that can be modified to help any student feel challenged and successful. Designing these experiences so they can be easily modified (through a different piece of equipment or a higher or lower number of repetitions to complete, or by giving students the power to challenge themselves) helps both with motivation and success.

Jump rope is a great example of an activity in which students can be challenged at their skill level. The following progression is one that I use with great success.

In the first grade, a continuous jump rope score is taken at the beginning of the year. Throughout the school year jump rope is used as both a station and a warm-up. A few weeks prior to Jump Rope for Heart, students' scores are again checked, and the students are challenged to make the Big 10 Club by having 10 continuous jumps. Any student who shows improvement gets an improvement award and continues to get improvement awards (on the CD, Level 2 Challenge\Activities\ Jump Rope Skill Challenge) until they make it into the Big 10. Students who make the Big 10 get a Big 10 award on the CD and sign the big poster in the gym that stays posted from March to June. At Jump Rope for Heart, they can sign Big 10 posters for jumping 10 continuous jumps backward, on one foot, and in a long rope.

Fitness goal sheet.

Big 10 Club and improvement awards.

level 2

challenge

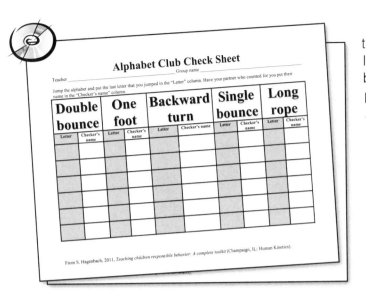

Check sheet for Alphabet Club.

The second grade has a similar system, but theirs is the Alphabet Club, and they jump to the letters of the alphabet in a variety of ways: forward, backward, one foot, single bounce (fast, hot peppers) and double bounce. If students complete the Alphabet Club Challenge, and time allows, they move on to tricks. I use an Alphabet check sheet at stations. During Jump Rope for Heart they are challenged with tricks they will need to know in third grade. The Alphabet check sheet and award are on the CD (Level 2 Challenge\Activities\Jump Rope Skill Challenge).

Third and fourth graders have three skill levels to challenge them. Each level has a direction element, foot patterns, a trick, partner challenges, and a long rope component. If they complete all three skill levels, they may try to master harder individual skills. Saving the skill level information from third grade provides a record so the student can start on the next level in fourth grade. Included on the CD are the third and fourth grade jump rope skill level sheets (Level 2 Challenge\Activities\ Jump Rope Skill Challenge). Students' partners check most skills by initialing when completed, but some skills (marked in boldface) must be checked by the teacher.

For students who struggle, you can lower the number of repetitions needed for passing the skill, require fewer skills for passing, or have the student jump over a stationary rope on the floor. For students who excel, there is always the next level or a harder individual skill to work on. Students work at their own level and progress as far as they can.

Having clear expectations helps with mastery and success. Students know the expectation: Most first graders can make it into the Big 10 club, most third graders can finish Level 1 in jump rope, and most fourth graders can complete Level 2 in jump

Award for Alphabet Club.

level 2

challenge

rope. Develop challenges and learning experiences that match your benchmarks and present them so students have a clear understanding.

○ BE A STAR DANCE

Dance is a great way to reinforce concepts and to get the heart pumping. The following dance is another activity that can be used to teach Level 2 Challenge for students in second through fourth grade. The story "Where Will You Be After PE?" tells students, "Challengers might not always be the brightest star, but they work responsibly, so they'll go far. They can take pride in everything they do, whether practicing old skills or learning new." All kids are born stars although some may shine brighter at different activities. The dance is to the song "A Star Is Born" from the Disney movie *Hercules*. It sends the message that all people are stars, and the way they challenge themselves will determine how brightly they will shine.

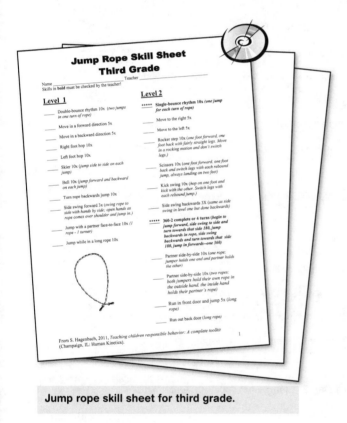

Jump rope skill sheet for third grade.

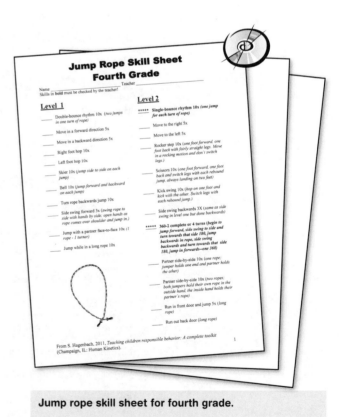

Jump rope skill sheet for fourth grade.

level 2

challenge

DANCE CUES FOR "A STAR IS BORN"

4 ct	March 4x
4 ct	Star jack—2 ct jump and make a star, 2 ct jump back together, "A star is born"
4 ct	March 4x
4 ct	Star jack, "A star is born"
16 ct	Lift knee and tap thigh every 2 ct 8x (alternate R L R L)
8 ct	March forward 4 steps, march backward 4 steps "A star is born"
4 ct	March 4x
4 ct	Star jack—2 ct jump and make a star, 2 ct jump back together "A star is born"
4 ct	March 4x
4 ct	Star jack, "A star is born"
16 ct	Lift knee and tap thigh every 2 ct 8x (alternate R L R L)
8 ct	Slide 4 ct to right and sweep arms up and then 4 ct sweep arms to other side
8 ct	Slide 4 ct to left and sweep arms up and then 4 ct sweep arms to other side
8 ct	March forward 4 steps to "Every night a star is" march back 4 steps
4 ct	March forward 4 steps, "Every night a star is"
8 ct	Six punches (high right, high left, low right, low left, high right, high left) and end in star jack
4 ct	March 4x
4 ct	Star jack—2 ct jump and make a star, 2 ct jump back together "A star is born"
4 ct	March 4x
4 ct	Star jack, "A star is born"
16 ct	Lift knee and tap thigh every 2 ct 8x (alternate R L R L)
8 ct	Slide 4 ct to right and sweep arms up and then 4 ct sweep arms to other side
8 ct	Slide 4 ct to left and sweep arms up and then 4 ct sweep arms to other side
8 ct	March forward 4 steps to "I'm telling you" march back 4 steps
4 ct	March 4x
4 ct	Star jack—2 ct jump and make a star, 2 ct jump back together "A star is born"
4 ct	March 4x
4 ct	Star jack, "A star is born"
16 ct	Lift knee and tap thigh every 2 ct 8x (alternate R L R L)
8 ct	Slide 4 ct to right and sweep arms up and then 4 ct sweep arms to other side
8 ct	Slide 4 ct to left and sweep arms up and then 4 ct sweep arms to other side
8 ct	March forward 4 steps to "Every night a star is" march back 4 steps
4 ct	March forward 4 steps, "Burning bright a star is"
8 ct	Six punches (high right, high left, low right, low left, high right, high left) and end in star jack

o CHALLENGE COACH

The Challenge Coach progression incorporates Standard 2 of the NASPE national standards (2004): "Demonstrates understanding of movement concepts, principles, strategies, and tactics as they apply to the learning and performance of physical activities." This activity engages students at varying levels of readiness and skills as they learn the challenge concepts through skill practice. Students are paired with a partner for one minute of continuous practice of a skill that you designate; one partner practices while the other acts as the challenge coach, giving feedback and encouragement to the practicing partner. Students may use the silly praise word they create while learning how to work at Level 3 Teamwork. (For kindergarten students, however, the challenge coach concept is not used; students practice on their own and assess their own practice using a quick thumb assessment.)

Equipment

- ▶ 1 one-minute sand timer per pair (or per student, for kindergarten students), or a stopwatch
- ▶ Whatever equipment is needed for the chosen skill (e.g., jump ropes or balls), 1 per pair (or one per student for kindergarten)
- ▶ Challenge Coach graph pieces (for grades 1 and 2; these and the other Challenge Coach materials are on the CD, Level 2 Challenge\Activities\Challenge Coach)
- ▶ Challenge Coach cards and focus cards for grades 3 and 4 (You can customize the focus card for whatever skill you want. Place it back to back with a Challenge Coach card in a sheet protector for each pair to use. You will be able to change focus cards for whatever skill you choose by simply switching the focus card in the sheet protector. Save these focus cards; you can use them again as a station to review a variety of skills.)
- ▶ Challenge Coach assessment (for grades 3 and 4)

Kindergarten

- ▶ *Focus*: Review the description of a Challenger. (A Challenger will think, think, think, and practice, practice, practice. If it is too easy, make it a challenge.) With this age group, focus on the concept of practice.
- ▶ *Description*: Assign a skill to practice and have students practice the skill continuously until the timer runs out. This may be done at a station where students can choose from two to four tasks to practice.
- ▶ *Reflection*: Students award themselves a thumbs-up if they practiced the whole time, a thumb-to-the-side if they practiced some of the time, and a thumbs-down if they should have practiced more.

First Grade

- ▶ *Focus*: Review the description of a Challenger. (A Challenger will think, think, think, and practice, practice, practice. If it is too easy, make it a challenge.) With this age group, focus on the concept of practice and thinking; don't yet emphasize increasing the challenge when it's too easy.

Challenge Coach card and focus card for grades 3 and 4.

level 2

challenge

Graph pieces for the Challenge Coach activity (grades 1-2).

From S. Hagembach, 2011, *Teaching children responsible behavior: A complete toolkit* (Champaign, IL: Human Kinetics).

▶ *Description*: Assign partners a skill to practice and a focus to think about. The teacher should assign the focus. One student is the player who practices the skill continuously until the timer runs out. The other student is the challenge coach whose job is to watch the player to see if she practices the entire time and thinks about the focus. Challenge coaches may only give positive, specific feedback. Students may use the silly praise word they create while learning how to work at Level 3 Teamwork. You should model this for students when introducing the activity. For example, you may say, "The task is to throw underhand to a target focusing on using an opposite foot step. The challenge coach watches for an opposite foot step and could comment, 'Nice opposite foot step' instead of 'Nice job.'" Students then switch roles. This may be done at a station where students can choose from two to four tasks to practice or for a specific skill assigned by the teacher.

▶ *Reflection*: Student can use the Challenge Coach graph (Level 2 Challenge\Activities\Challenge Coach) or use the thumb system. Have them give a thumbs-up if they practiced the whole time, thumbs-to-the-side if they practiced some of the time, thumbs-down if they should have practiced more. You could also ask if they were thinking about the designated focus.

Second Grade

▶ *Focus*: Review the definition of a Challenger. (A Challenger will think, think, think, and practice, practice, practice. If it is too easy, make it a challenge.) With this age group, focus on the concept of practice and thinking. Later in the year, if they are ready, you can emphasize adding a challenge if the task is too easy. If you choose to add this focus, be sure to review how to create a challenge and the characteristics of a challenge.

▶ *Description*: Assign partners a skill to practice and a few focus points to think about. One student is the player who practices a skill continuously until the timer runs out and chooses what he will focus on. The other student is the challenge coach whose job is to watch the player to see if he practices the entire time and thinks about the focus chosen. Challenge coaches may give only positive, specific feedback. Students may use the silly praise word they create while learning how to work at Level 3 Teamwork. You should model this for students when introducing the activity. For example, you may say, "The task is to throw underhand to a target focusing on using an opposite foot step and T-stretch. The challenge coach watches for an opposite foot step and T-stretch. When she sees one, she may say, 'Nice opposite foot step' or "Great T-stretch" instead of 'Nice Job.'" Students then switch jobs. This may be done at a station where students can choose from two to four tasks to practice or for a specific skill assigned by the teacher.

Some students will not make the task more challenging because it is already a challenge. When you add the third focus—making the task more challenging if it's too easy—challenge coaches will need to understand that. To help students understand this concept, have the challenge coach ask the player, "Was the task

level 2

challenge

a challenge?" If the response is no, the challenge coach may ask, "How did you make it a challenge?"

▶ *Reflection*: Use the Challenge Coach graph or use the modified Challenge Coach student assessment, both on the CD (Level 2 Challenge\Activities\Challenge Coach). Let students know to fill in the face with a smile if the player met the criteria most of the time, a straight face for some of the time, and a frown if she needs to improve.

Third and Fourth Grade

▶ *Focus*: Review the definition of a Challenger. (A Challenger will think, think, think, and practice, practice, practice. If it is too easy, make it a challenge.) With this age group, focus on all the concepts of challenge: practice, thinking, and making the task more difficult if it becomes easy. Also review how to create a challenge and the characteristics of a challenge (posters relating to these concepts are on the CD, Level 2 Challenge\Posters).

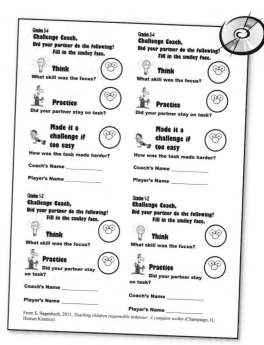

Assessment for the Challenge Coach activity.

▶ *Description*: This may be done as a station activity or all-class activity. I tend to teach the skill, and then use the Challenge Coach activity in a station or as an all-class review before skill testing. Pair the students: One will be the challenge coach and the other student, the player. Give each pair a timer and a Challenge Coach Card (sheet protector with the Challenge Coach card back-to-back with the teacher-generated focus card). The pair should see the focus card side. The coach will need to ask the player what the player will focus on while she practices the skill. At this level, depending on the skill, players may choose to work on more than one focus which is, in itself, a type of a challenge. During the one- or two-minute practice time, the challenge coach should give positive, specific feedback on the focus or foci chosen by the player. At the end of the one or two minutes, the coach and player switch roles. This works well with volleyball. The challenge coach can toss the ball to the player to strike for the allotted time and give positive feedback on the skill. In basketball the challenge coach can be the rebounder.

▶ *Reflection*: The Challenge Coach student assessment is on the CD (Level 2 Challenge\Activities\Challenge Coach). I use this more often when I use the Challenge Coach activity as a review of a skill. Let students know to fill in the face with a smile if the player met the criteria most of the time, a straight face for some of the time, and a frown if she needs to improve.

Reflecting on Level 2 Challenge

On days where skill practice is a focus, you can use the Challenge Graph as a reflective activity at the end of class to see if students challenged themselves. Graph pieces are on the CD (Level 2 Challenge\Activities\Challenge Coach). Place the three headings, Think, Practice, and Challenge, in the top pocket. Make 12 to 18 Challenger Graph chips. Place these chips under the correct heading as students explain how they were at Level 2 Challenge. A student may name a focus point he thought of during class. You would place a chip under the Think heading. A student may

level 2

challenge

explain how she changed the task to make it a challenge. You would then place a chip under the challenge heading.

You can also use the thumbs-up assessment at the end of class to encourage student reflection about where they were during class. Thumbs-up means they showed Level 2 Challenge most of the time during class, thumbs-to-the-side means they showed Level 2 some of the time, and thumbs-down means they need to work harder at Level 2. Students may also touch a level poster on the way out of the gym to show what levels they were working at during class. There are two different level posters on the CD in the All Levels folder that could be displayed.

There are five homework activities on the CD (Level 2 Challenge\Reflection\ Homework and Assessments). The homework activities can be used by classroom teachers who incorporate the levels into the classroom or have the responsibility of teaching physical education. Physical education teachers can use them on days when they are asked to give up their teaching space for special events, or they can use them as assessments. They may also be used to reinforce the concepts taught in class as physical education homework.

Younger students in kindergarten and first grade may draw a picture of what they would like to improve or circle the Challenger in a strip of pictures. There is also a word search activity for students in second grade and a crossword puzzle for students in grades three or four that reinforces ways of creating challenges. A reflective piece that asks students in grades three and four how to show Level 2 Challenge all day long is another option.

The reader for Level 2 Challenge is titled "Olympic Challengers." One of the stories is about the most famous Olympic athlete to come in last, John Stephen Akhwari, who completed the Olympic marathon despite being injured. The moral of the athlete biographies is that you do not have to win to be a Challenger. The reader can be used in the classroom, as homework, or in physical education. It is on the CD (Level 2 Challenge\Reflection\Reader).

Once all three levels have been introduced and practiced, students may periodically fill out a How Are You Doing assessment on the CD in the All Levels folder. There is a simple one that students fill in with a smile, straight face, or frown and an advanced one that students complete by looking at outcomes specified by the national standards and checking those they have achieved.

From S. Hagenbach, 2011, *Teaching children responsible behavior: A complete toolkit* (Champaign, IL: Human Kinetics).

Level touch chart.

level 2

challenge

Level touch target poster.

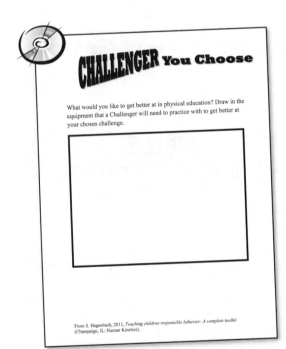

Draw a picture of what you would like to improve.

Find and circle the Challenger.

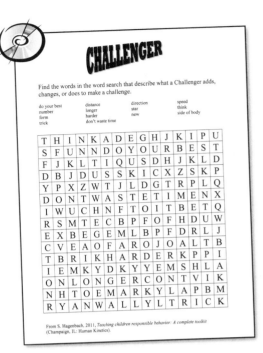

Challenge Word Search activity.

Key for Challenge Word Search activity.

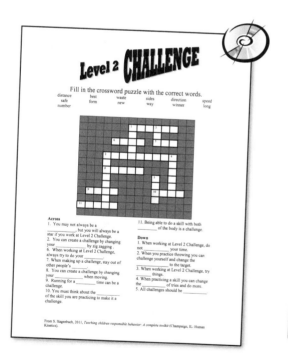

Challenge Crossword activity.

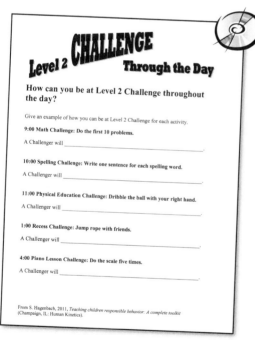

Challenge All Day activity.

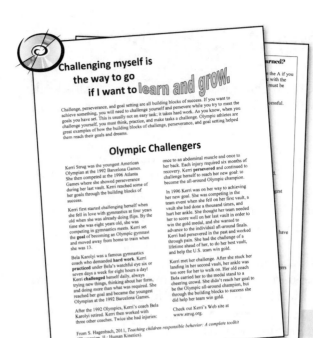

Challenge reader.

How Are You Doing assessment for grades K to 2.

How Are You Doing assessment for grades 3 and 4.

Communicating With Parents

Part of effective teaching is setting clear expectations for your students. This leads to more effective learning and helps create a positive learning environment. Parents should also know your expectations. They will be interested in what their children are learning.

On the CD are two letters you can send to parents for this unit: one explaining the three levels (in the All Levels folder) and another discussing the Challenger story (Level 2 Challenge\Communication). A pledge sheet for the student to sign may be put on the back of the parent letter. This gives the student the power to choose to be a Challenger. There is power in choice and with it comes the feeling of satisfaction for doing the right things. Rewards for doing well are not necessary.

Another communication tool is the Elementary Physical Education Progress Report based on the NASPE national standards and outcomes on the CD in the All Levels folder. You may use either the *concern* report or the *excelling* report as needed to inform parents of their children's progress between grading periods. This will help avoid surprises to parents at grading periods.

Parent note explaining the Challenger story and student pledge.

level 2

challenge

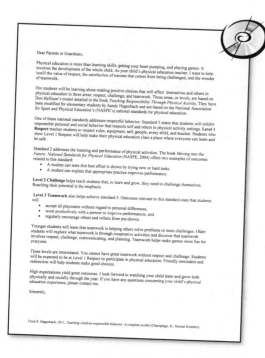

Parent note explaining the three levels.

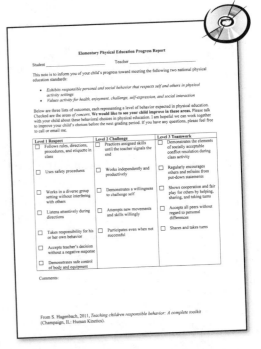

Progress report for students who are doing well.

Supporting Standards and Performance Outcomes

All of our activities and lesson designs should support our standards, benchmarks, and outcomes. The following three national standards (NASPE 2004) are met through Level 2 Challenge:

Standard 2: Demonstrates understanding of movement concepts, principles, strategies, and tactics as they apply to the learning and performance of physical activities.

Standard 5: Exhibits responsible personal and social behavior that respects self and others in physical activity settings.

Standard 6: Values physical activity for health, enjoyment, challenge, self-expression, and social interaction.

Some performance outcomes (NASPE 2004) are listed here as examples of those that relate to challenge.

With each sample outcome, I have also included some corresponding child-friendly learning targets written as *I can* statements that refer to challenge in terms of the standards and outcomes. The push in our district, as it is in education nationally, is to provide students with learning targets, in the belief that students learn more if they know what they are expected to learn. These targets should be written in child-friendly language

Progress report for students who need improvement.

level 2

challenge

and should be posted in the classroom. You should address these targets at some time in your lesson. We strive to post our learning targets in every subject: math, reading, physical education, art, music, social studies, and science.

States that best effort is shown by trying new or hard tasks.
– *I can try new or hard tasks to show my best effort.*

Explains that appropriate practice improves performance.
– *I can think, practice, and make a task a challenge to improve my skills.*

Accurately recognizes the critical elements of a skill made by a fellow student and provides feedback to that student.
– *I can be a challenge coach.*

Willingly tries new movements and skills.
– *I can challenge myself by trying new skills.*

Continues to participate when not successful on the first try.
– *I can keep working on a skill when I am not successful.*

Selects and practices a skill on which improvement is needed.
– *I can create challenges that will improve my skills.*

– *I can set a goal, practice and reach it.*

Interacts with others by helping with their physical activity challenges.
– *I can help others with their challenge.*

Practices specific skills as assigned until the teacher signals the end of practice.
– *I can practice, practice, practice in physical education.*

Work productively with a partner to improve performance.
– *I can be a challenge coach.*

Summary

Level 2 Challenge is the teaching level. This is where you get to be creative by differentiating your instruction so all your students can be successful Challengers. It is a wonderful gift you will give your students—learning how they can challenge themselves, set goals, and achieve them by thinking, practicing, and persevering until they are reached.

level 2

challenge

Where Will You Be After PE?

Sandy Hagenbach

You must challenge yourself to learn and grow;
this is something that Wasters don't know.
Challengers want to be their best,
so they work harder than all the rest!

Wasters waste their time all day;
all they want to do is play.
They don't take responsibility
for their learning, as you will see.

Change the distance.

When they master a skill, Challengers won't rest.
They'll make the skill harder so they can be the best.
But Wasters just want to make lots of bull's-eyes,
So they stay close to the target, where it's easy as pie.

After PE you will hear a Waster say . . .

"Oh, bummer!
He gets to throw a big touchdown,
while I get to hand the water around."

Think about your form.

When Challengers practice their throwing movements,
they think about form and aim for improvement.
Wasters don't think as they're throwing around;
they waste time goofing off and acting like clowns.

After PE you will hear a Waster say . . .

"Oh, bummer!
She's in the game making big plays,
while I'm just standing here catching some rays."

Try new things.

Challengers try old things in ways that are new;
they always want to see what else they can do.
Wasters are content with the same old stuff,
so they spend class time talking, not trying anything tough.

After PE you will hear a Waster say . . .

"Oh, bummer!
He's the one who shows he can jump,
while I sit and watch on my big round rump."

Push yourself— how long can you go?

Challengers want to keep moving along,
so they pace themselves to make their heart strong.
Wasters make excuses to stop and rest;
they don't try to do their very best.

After PE you will hear a Waster say . . .

"Oh, bummer!
She can run and play all day long,
while I must rest because my heart's not that strong."

Use both sides of the body.

Challengers practice with both of their sides;
they refine their skills through hard work and pride.
Wasters don't use their opposite hand;
they're content just to do what they already can.

After PE you will hear a Waster say . . .

"She's the one who's shooting lights out—
but maybe I'm starting to figure things out."

Change direction.

It's easy to dribble in a straight line,
but zigging and zagging and dodging take time.
Challengers practice when Wasters play,
so Challengers become more skilled every day.

After PE you will hear a Waster say . . .

"He's the hero who scores from a steal,
while I want to have that 'I did it!' feel."

Increase the number.

Doing more than the teacher asks
is one way Challengers get better at tasks.
They push themselves harder and try to do more,
making sure to do skills with excellent form.

After PE you will hear a new **CHALLENGER** say . . .

"Did you see how long she hung from the bar?
I can do that—I'll practice and go far!"

Challengers might not always be the brightest star,
but they work responsibly, so they'll go far.
They can take pride in everything they do,
whether practicing old skills or learning new.

Wasters can change; they just need to work harder
to become Challengers and make themselves prouder.
All of us are born to be stars;
our choices determine how bright we are.

Think, practice, challenge is what you can do
to show the star that's inside you.
Taking responsibility for our choices is what we need
to be Challengers who most certainly will succeed.

* ★ Think about your form.
* ★ Change the distance.
* ★ Push—how long can you go?
* ★ Use both sides of the body.
* ★ Change direction.
* ★ Try new things.
* ★ Increase the number.

After PE you will hear yourself say . . .

"Being responsible is right for me,
there is no stopping what I can be!
Challenging myself is the way to go
if I want to learn and grow.
I have the choice to be the best I can be
in life, in class, and in PE!"

Teamwork

Level 3 Teamwork is the level that will give students the skills to work in a team. Many are the same skills children need to develop friendships. Being a friend is an important focus for the younger student. Students in physical education have so many opportunities to interact with classmates, which makes learning friendship skills to build teamwork essential. In this book, teamwork for younger students is defined as Friendlies helping others solve problems or meet challenges. Students need to be able to work with others as Friendlies before true teamwork can occur. The story "Who Will You Be in PE?" helps young students visualize what being a friend looks like. The two main characters are Friendlies, who always think of others, and I-MEs who only think of themselves. The Friendlies have a "Golden Rule" glow while the I-MEs are a little green with envy.

Once students have heard the story "Who Will You Be in PE?" and have done the activities in this chapter, they will need consistent reinforcement of the concept of being a Friendly. Find teachable moments and try to set them in a positive light. For example, imagine you see two students fighting over a hula hoop. You can re-enact the situation and ask, "What would a Friendly do?" Try not to ask, "Who is the I-ME?"

Perhaps you hear a student criticizing another student. Stop the class and discuss how the students can be Friendlies by making people feel good about themselves. Ask them if they remember their special praise phrase. Or perhaps you can make up a special praise phrase to use for the rest of class period. Keep your students thinking, and be positive.

As students mature, the definition of teamwork becomes more detailed and includes a statement about needing a plan. Students can collaborate and create a class definition of teamwork after observing a team in action. A class definition of teamwork makes it more personal and hopefully more meaningful.

Children's Story

"Who Will You Be in PE?" is a pattern story. First the students will see the I-MEs in action with the heading, "I-MEs think only of themselves" at the top of the page. On the opposite page, the Friendlies appear with the heading, "Friendlies think of others—they care," and a summary at the bottom of the page. The following two pages ask the students, "Who Will You Be in PE?" Encourage students to join in and read this page with you each time it appears.

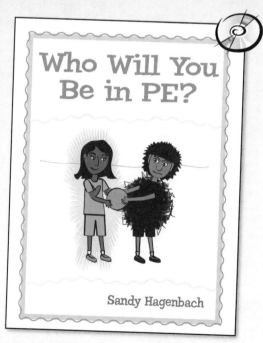

Who Will You Be in PE?

Sandy Hagenbach

"Who Will You Be in PE?" is on page 143 and the CD.

As I developed the stories, I got input from our school's reading specialist, Alissa Roe. She pointed out it would be best to read the heading at the top of the page, which is the main point, then read the speaking bubbles. Repeat this pattern on the Friendlies' page and end with the summary at the bottom. Reinforce the idea that being a friend is shown through actions that one chooses.

The YMCA Red Heart Core Value of Caring is the focus of this story. Young children involved in YMCA programs will be able to learn what caring is by listening to the story. Then, by participating in the activities found in the teamwork unit, they can feel what caring is. Teaching values through a story and action makes learning fun and effective.

Introducing Level 3 Teamwork

The following activities can be used with the story to reinforce the concepts taught in this book.

o COMMON MIXER

Equipment

▶ Music

Description

This activity reinforces the concept that Friendlies are friends to everyone. Have students scattered in the general space. Give the students instructions for how they should move (perhaps skipping or hopping) and start playing some music. Stop the music and call out an action, such as "shake hands." The students should find a partner and perform the action. Then instruct them in a new way to move and start the music again. When the music stops, the students find a new partner and follow the new instruction, such as "High five your partner." After the students have responded with three different partners, the teacher may repeat the calls, and students must always go to the partner they first did the actions with.

Example: Sue is always Ben's shaking hand partner.
Sue is always Joe's high five partner.
Ben is always Joe's low five partner.

Below is a list of possible calls.

Handshake	Rock-Paper-Scissors	Knuckles
Elbow to elbow	Low five	Thumbs-up
High five	Toe-to-toe	Do-si-do
Curl	Shoulder touches	Stare down
Bouncing	Back-to-back	Big pumpkin grin

o TEAMS ADD UP

Equipment

▶ 12 to 14 hoops
▶ Music

level 3

teamwork

Description

By making sure everyone is included, this activity teaches students that Friendlies are friends to everyone. Scatter hoops on the floor and instruct the students to perform a specific locomotor skill while avoiding the hoops. When the music stops, call out two different body parts and a specific quantity of each part, such as five feet and three hands. Students gather in groups to put the specified number of body parts into the hoops, in this case, five feet and three hands. This combination could be made with a group as small as three students and as large as eight students. This is a great way to incorporate some math integration too!

o PARTNER DANCE

Equipment

▶ *Handy Manny* CD
▶ Music player

Description

Partner dances are a great way to teach children how to be a friend to everyone. This is a slow dance to a great song, "Amigos Forever" from the *Handy Manny* CD. It is appropriate for kindergarten through second grade. Remind students to be friends with everyone showing them respect. Remember to respect every child and don't go wild.

To begin the dance form two lines with partners facing each other. Lines should be approximately eight steps apart. Practice showing respect to every child, by practicing the patty cake and partner turn before teaching the steps to the dance.

16 ct	Intro	Sway arms every 2 ct L, R, L, R
16 ct	4x	4 ct, side step L, together, L, together, and clap; repeat to R, L, R
16 ct	2x	4 ct, walk forward and give partner a high five 4 ct, walk back
16 ct	4x	4 ct side step L, together, L, together and clap; repeat to R, L, R
4 ct	Chorus	Walk forward
4 ct	Chorus	Patty cake, "Amigos," high knees, "for," clap hands, "ever," clap partner's hands
8 ct	Chorus	Join hands and circle
4 ct	Chorus	Patty cake, "Working," hit knees, "to" clap hands, "gether," clap partner's hands
4 ct	Chorus	Patty cake, "It's such," hit knees, "a," clap hands, "pleasure," clap partner's hands
8 ct	Chorus	Join hands and circle (to mix it up this can be a do-si-do or an elbow swing)
16 ct	Music	Sway arms every 2 ct L, R, L, R, and back up
16 ct	4x	4 ct, side step L, together, L, together, and clap; repeat to R, L, R
16 ct	2x	4 ct, walk forward and high five partner, 4 ct walk back
16 ct	4x	4 ct, side step L, together, L, together, and clap; repeat to R, L, R

(continued)

level 3

teamwork

(continued)

4 ct	Chorus	Walk forward
4 ct	Chorus	Patty cake, "Amigos," hit knees, "for," clap hands, "ever," clap partner's hands
8 ct	Chorus	Join hands and circle
4 ct	Chorus	Patty cake, "Working," hit knees, "to," clap hands, "gether," clap partner's hands
4 ct	Chorus	Patty cake, "It's such," hit knees, "a" clap hands, "pleasure," clap partner's hands
8 ct	Chorus	Join hands and circle (to mix it up, this can be a do-si-do or an elbow swing)
16 ct	Music	Sway arms every 2 ct, L, R, L, R, and back up
I sometimes stop the dance here if I want to do another activity.		
32 ct	Chorus	Repeat chorus pattern
32 ct	Chorus	Repeat chorus pattern—First 4 cts are a patty cake not a walk forward
32 ct	Chorus	Repeat chorus pattern—First 4 cts are a patty cake not a walk forward

○ ROCK-PAPER-SCISSORS

This activity reinforces the concept that Friendlies compromise. Explain the game of Rock-Paper-Scissors: A rock (fist) squishes scissors (two fingers apart) for a win, paper (hand held flat) covers the rock for a win, and scissors cuts the paper for a win. I use the cue, "Think . . . 1, 2, show." On "show," each student shows a fist for rock, a flat hand for paper, or fingers apart for scissors. I found that when the cue was, "Rock-paper-scissors, show," some kindergarteners would always show scissors; they were following the call precisely. Before playing Puppies and Penguins, have the students practice "Think.....1, 2, show". Then you may have the class try to beat the teacher. Students show either Rock-Paper-Scissors and compare it to the teacher's choice. Once students understand the Rock-Paper-Scissors game the class is ready to play Puppies and Penguins.

○ PUPPIES AND PENGUINS

Play music; when it stops, students quickly find a nearby partner and play Rock-Paper-Scissors. The winner stays standing to become a penguin, while the person who lost kneels down to become a puppy. While music is on, students move as the animal or character that they represent. When the music stops, each penguin partners with another penguin, puppies pair with other puppies, and each pair plays Rock-Paper-Scissors. The puppy that wins becomes a penguin, and a penguin that loses becomes a puppy. Play just one game to win; never the best out of three!

Name changes for Puppies and Penguins.

Ghosts and spiders	Whales and crabs	Elves and reindeer
Cranes and bulldozers	Tiggers and Eeyores	Foxes and rabbits

level 3

teamwork

o PRAISE PHRASE

Equipment

▶ Something to write on, such as a marker board and markers

Description

This activity reinforces the concept that Friendlies make other people feel good. Help students list words that make people feel good. Suggest or elicit *praise* words such as great, awesome, super, fantastic, wow, fabulous, nice, or good. Let students experiment and combine two words to form a new word.

Fantastic + fabulous = fantabulous	Nice + rocking = nocking
Wow + great = wreat	Wow + awesome = wowsome
Nice + super = nuper	Super + nice = supice
Fantastic + awesome = fansome	Great + super = greaper

Keep a list and choose a silly praise word for the day or have a special word for each class. A special homework sheet decoding silly praise phrases is included on the CD. These silly praise words can be used with the Challenge Coach activity from Teaching Level 2 Challenge (page 91). Hint: don't put *nice* and *good* together; you will get *nood* and it may sound like *nude*!

o PRAISE PHRASE STATIONS

Once the class has created their praise phrase, have students choose partners. You may want to do the Common Mixer activity (page 122). Give students a variety of challenges to perform at stations and have students praise their partners with the silly praise word of the day when they meet the challenge. No negative comments allowed! This activity can be combined with Taking-Turns Stations.

o TAKING-TURNS STATIONS

Equipment

▶ 1 or 2 scooters

▶ 1 or 2 hippity-hop balls

▶ A container with a few catching choices (Koosh ball, beanbag, yarn ball)

▶ Long jump rope

▶ 2 basketballs

▶ 3 cones

▶ A climbing station (rope, cargo net, or a wall)

▶ A balance beam

▶ 2 playground balls

▶ A yarn ball or nerf ball

▶ Bowling pins for targets

▶ A wall target

level 3

teamwork

Description

This activity reinforces the concept that Friendlies take turns. Review Rock-Paper-Scissors. Remind students that if they are not sure who should go first the first time, they can compromise and do Rock-Paper-Scissors.

Set up six to eight stations. Divide the class into groups of two or three. At each station have an activity where students must wait and take a turn. This activity can be combined with having the Friendlies make others feel good. Have the student waiting give the original class praise word. You may choose to have something for the students to do during the time they are waiting. As students change stations, a different person should go first.

TURN STATIONS	WAITING OPTIONS
Ride the scooter to the cone and back	Play catch alone with an object from a choice basket
Jump in a long rope	Help turn the jump rope
Ride the hippity-hop ball to the cone and back	Play catch alone with an object from a choice basket
Climb (rope, cargo net, wall)	Jump rope, hold the cargo net, or spot the player
Throw at a target	Play catch with a partner or against the wall
Kick to a target	Play catch with a partner or against the wall
Roll to a target	Stand by target to reset
Shoot at basket	Dribble in place
Dribble to a cone and back	Dribble in place
Walk across a beam	Shoulder touches

○ SHARE AND CATCH RELAY

Equipment

- ▶ Playground ball
- ▶ Beanbag
- ▶ Yarn ball
- ▶ Koosh ball
- ▶ Music

Description

This activity reinforces taking turns and lining up politely. Divide class into teams of 4-6 students per team. I use my squad groups to form the teams. Each team starts in a circle and plays catch with a ball to music. (I use a different piece of equipment for each game, such as a playground ball, beanbag, yarn ball, and Koosh ball.) While waiting to catch a ball, the students have hands in a ready position. Once they have caught and thrown the ball, they put their hands behind their backs. This lets everyone know who has or has not had a turn. When everyone has had a turn to throw and catch, all the children on the team puts their hands in a ready position again. When the music stops, the team quickly forms a line and passes the ball over their heads

level 3

teamwork

to the end of the line. Choose how many times each person must touch the ball. This will make each team member go to the end of the line after touching the ball. I usually do this once for kindergarten, twice for first grade, and two to three times for second grade. When they have touched the ball the designated number of times, the student sits down. Demonstrate once as Friendlies (going to the end of line with no pushing or shoving) and once as I-MEs (arguing about wanting to be the first person to line up behind the ball holder). Discuss what they saw.

o GOOD SPORTS AROUND THE TOWN

Equipment
- ▶ 9 to 12 ice cream pails with 9 to 12 beanbags
- ▶ 9 to 12 five-pound tin cans with 9 to 12 Koosh balls
- ▶ 6 to 12 poly spots with 6 to 12 beanbags
- ▶ 6 to 12 laundry baskets with 6 to 12 Koosh balls

Description

This activity reinforces the concept that Friendlies don't brag; instead, they compliment others. For this activity you will need one station for every pair of students. Each station is exactly the same and has a set of two to four targets set up like Bozo buckets. I use poly spots, five-pound tin cans, ice cream pails, and laundry baskets for targets, and beanbags or Koosh balls to throw. (You may be able to get the tin cans from your food service. I send home a note periodically asking for recyclables, and specify ice cream pails as something I'd like.) Set up fewer targets for kindergarteners and more for first or second graders. You may give each target a point value for second grade. For kindergarten and first grade, each target is worth one point. I usually have students throw a beanbag at each target. They have three throws in each turn and must throw to each bucket, starting with the closest and ending with the farthest. Students take turns throwing, adding up their points for one round. If there is a tie, they play a second round. If there is still a tie, they do Rock-Paper-Scissors to decide a winner. If the pair is done playing and have decided on the winner, they may continue to play until the class is ready to rotate.

Before the class rotates, students may shake hands, give a high five, or give *knucks* to their partners and congratulate them. Winners move to the right; others stay at their station. This is somewhat like a Bunco rotation. Pick one station to be the top station. At the top station the winner stays put and the other person moves to the right. Put emphasis on the congratulations part of the rotation. The class silly praise word can be used at this time.

o TEAM SCOOP

Equipment
- ▶ 6 buckets or baskets to hold scooped objects (3 for each team)
- ▶ 12 to 14 scoops (one for every 2 students)
- ▶ 15 to 20 blue objects that could be scooped up
- ▶ 30 to 40 objects of other colors (such as tennis balls, waffle balls, beanbags, Koosh balls)

level 3

teamwork

Description

This activity reinforces the concept that Friendlies share, are helpful, and use teamwork. This is a modified game of Scoop 'Em Up found in Grineski's (1996) *Cooperative Learning in Physical Education*. Scatter colorful balls and beanbags on the floor, making sure there are fewer blue objects. Divide the class into two teams: Friendlies and I-MEs. Have each team select partners, give each partnership a scoop, and assign each of them a basket, set off to the side, for holding their scooped objects. Have all the I-MEs' baskets on one side of the gym, and all the Friendlies' baskets on the opposite side. Partners join hands with one person holding the scoop.

When the music starts, each pair goes to the center of the gym to pick up a ball or beanbag. I-MEs are selfish and want only blue objects. Friendlies share and don't care what color they pick up. The partner with the scoop uses it to pick up a ball or beanbag.

Friendly partners may assist with the scoop up because Friendlies are helpful. I-MEs may not help their partner. Once an object is retrieved, it is carried to the pair's basket and dropped in. After each drop in the basket, the scoop is transferred to the other partner.

At the end of the game, have Friendlies and I-MEs count up their equipment. Compare the numbers. Play the game again and have teams switch roles, with I-MEs becoming Friendlies and vice versa.

Based on S. Grineski, 1996, *Cooperative learning in physical education* (Champaign, IL: Human Kinetics).

o CONFLICT RESOLUTION

About midyear, I take a day to introduce the second grade to a method of conflict resolution called Using the Levels to Solve Problems. With this method, students collaborate and work through the levels to resolve conflicts. At Level 1 Respect, you state the problem. Move to Level 2 Challenge and brainstorm solutions to the problem. Then use Level 3 Teamwork to choose the solution that is best for all. Using this method will help students make connections, practice communication skills, and collaborate to find an acceptable solution to conflicts.

Introduce the concept with the Using the Levels to Solve Problems poster (on the CD, Level 3 Teamwork\Posters). Choose one of the following scenarios to use as an example for the class. I begin by reading a scenario and then ask the class to identify the problem and name a few solutions. Once we have a few solutions, we choose one that is best for all. The following are some scenarios to consider.

Your squad is switching stations when both Franklin and Latisha pick up the same jump rope. They begin pulling on the rope and started arguing about who got to the rope first.

Henry starts to play catch with Iben, and Frank stops them and says he wants to be Henry's partner. Frank says Iben always plays with Henry. Iben says that is not true!

Yen has been first the last three times Wilma and Yen had to share a scooter. Wilma wants to go first, and Yen won't get off of the scooter.

Connie is following Birgit on an obstacle course and keeps trying to pass her. Birgit is getting angry and puts her arm out to block Connie from passing. Connie says Birgit is pushing her!

Doris says Colleen cut in front of her when they went to line up at the end of class. Colleen says they both got to the line at the same time.

Ahmed and Zubin are playing kick ball. Ahmed boots the ball near first base. Zubin calls it foul, and Ahmed says it is good.

level 3

teamwork

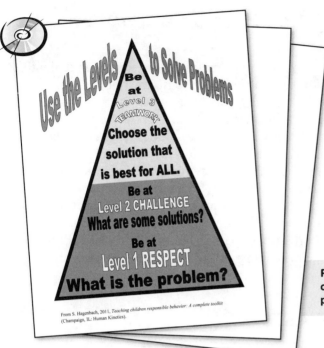

From S. Hagenbach, 2011, *Teaching children responsible behavior: A complete toolkit* (Champaign, IL: Human Kinetics).

Poster to use when introducing the concept of using the levels to solve problems.

Lavon tags Monique, and Monique keeps running. Lavon says he tagged Monique, and Monique says she never felt the tag.

Hans, Leasha, and Lars are shooting free throws to see who can get the most in a row. Hans says Leasha stepped over the line. Leasha says she was behind the line. Lars wasn't watching Leasha's feet; he just knows she made the free throw.

After modeling for the class the process of using the levels to solve problems, divide the class into four to six groups and give them each a scenario. I also laminate a copy of the Using the Levels to Solve Problems poster for each group to use as a guide. The groups practice the conflict resolution method and act out the scenarios for the class using the method modeled by the teacher.

I don't use any equipment for this lesson. I want the students to be creative and use everyone in the group either as props or as narrators. For example, in the catching scenario, while Henry and Iben are playing catch, the ball may be a student who moves back and forth between the two characters. In the jump rope scenario, students may act as the jump ropes and lie on the ground. Some students have a tendency to get a little silly with this lesson; in that case, remind them to work at Level 1 Respect.

I keep the individual laminated copies of the Using the Levels to Solve Problems poster on my cart. When students need help resolving a conflict, I give them the card to use as a reference. The group with the conflict must move out of the activity area and resolve their conflict. Once resolved, they put the card on my cart and return to the activity. If they have trouble resolving the conflict, I will ask them if they want a friend or the teacher to help.

This conflict resolution method can then be reviewed in a station activity for third and fourth graders. I have students pair up at a station, giving each pair a poster card. They choose a scenario out of a pail and discuss how to resolve the situation using the levels. Once the scenario problem is resolved, students choose another scenario. When you use this as a station activity, try to have a very active station that follows. You may also discuss a scenario at the end of class during the closure part of your lesson as a review.

level 3

teamwork

Reinforcing Level 3 Teamwork

Any time students are working with partners or on teams, look for teachable moments to reinforce Level 3 Teamwork. Prior to the activity, reinforce concepts that may be an issue such as sharing balls in a throwing game. Watch for students being at Level 3 Teamwork and point out their good choices.

Parachute play is a great team activity for younger students. It lets a class of Friendlies help each other meet a challenge. Another way of teaching students how to help others meet challenges is through playing games of catch, forming letters of the alphabet with a partner using their bodies, or making words with jump ropes. My first graders learn about flexibility by making different alphabet shapes with their own body. Once they have mastered a few letters as individuals, I challenge them to use teamwork. A student who is being a Friendly and helping another student meet the challenge of making alphabet shapes with a partner is at Level 3 Teamwork.

○ WINTER WONDERLAND

Equipment

▶ 30 or 35 snowballs (e.g., white shower scrubbies or beanbags)

Description

This is a direction game where each direction has a different action, and the teacher randomly calls out directions (see table below). Scatter snowballs around the gym: Snowballs may be beanbags, but I use white shower scrubbies. (White shower scrubbies are another item to add to your parent note when you ask for extra manipulatives

Direction	Movement response
Snowball	Self toss and play catch with snowball that is on floor
Snow shoe	Walk like you are wearing snow shoes
Snowplow	Scoot on your bottom with hands up like on a steering wheel; don't plow up snow
Snow angel	Jumping jacks
Snowman	Three people in a row: one sitting, one at ready position, and one standing; don't touch others
Snow shovel	Shoulder touches in a push-up position, pretending to throw snow over shoulders
Snowball fight	Play catch with a partner, throw ball to, not at, your partner
Snow fort	Two people join hands and raise them to make a roof; you can also let a student sit in the snow fort
Snowmobile	Two people: back person puts hands on front person's shoulders and both shuffle their feet (feet are the skis and cannot leave floor)
Snowboard	Slide with knees bent and arms out like on a snowbord

level 3

teamwork

and recyclables. Make sure to note you only want new white ones.) I teach this before Jack Frost tag so they learn the concept of working together to build a snowman.

○ JACK FROST TAG

Equipment

▶ Tagging implement (e.g., white shower scrubbie as a snowball)

Description

I post this definition of teamwork in the gym: "Teamwork is a friendly helping someone solve a problem or meet a challenge." This concept is easily reinforced with any cooperative tag game that involves rescuing a tagged classmate who is frozen or caught. Jack Frost Tag is a fun tag game. One student is Jack Frost. Students stand on an end line then count off and become either an ice storm or blizzard. Jack Frost stands past the closest free throw line in the half circle, his igloo, and calls out either blizzard or ice storm, and the group called runs across the gym trying not to get tagged by Jack Frost. If they are tagged, fall down, go out of bounds, or crash, they become frozen in the "ready" position. To save the frozen student, their teammates must complete a snowman: One classmate sits in front of the frozen student and another classmate stands behind the frozen student. Then all three join hands in a line and walk with their teammates to the side of the gym that students were running to. The tagger should not call out blizzard or ice storm if a snowman is walking towards the group.

○ OCEAN KINGDOM

Equipment

▶ 2 deck rings per pair of students or 2 plastic flying discs
▶ Hula hoop for each pair of students
▶ Sea creatures or a variety of equipment representing sea creatures (tennis balls, Koosh balls, beanbags, yarn balls, Nerf balls)
▶ 2 or 3 scooters
▶ 2 or 3 pipe insulation foam tubes
▶ Taggers
▶ Music (I like to use "Under the Sea" from Disney's *The Little Mermaid*)

Description

This game is appropriate for first through third grade. Students are paired and have two deck rings or flying discs. Instead of holding hands, they connect by holding the deck ring or disc. A hula hoop or basket is placed on the floor on one side of the gym; each pair of students will place their captured sea creatures there. I use sea creature beanie babies that I've purchased at the Dollar Store or rummage sales. Scatter sea creatures (or beanbags, fluff balls, yarn balls, spider balls) on the opposite side of the gym. Leave room between hoops and creatures for taggers to scoot on scooters. Two taggers sit on scooters as the ocean king and queen. Taggers hold pipe insulation representing tridents that will be used to tag pairs of students who have captured a sea creature.

level 3

teamwork

When the music starts playing, students try to collect as many sea creatures as possible without getting tagged and place them in their hula hoops. Students must stay connected by holding on to the deck ring or disc. Using the deck ring or disc, students squeeze and lift a sea creature and take it back to their hula hoop. Students should be at Level 1 Respect for rules and pick up only one sea creature at a time. If students drop a sea creature, they leave it where it lies and return to their hula hoop to do a designated activity, such as 10 shoulder touches or 10 jumping jacks, and then start collecting again. If they are tagged by the king or queen, they must drop their sea creature and return to their hula hoop to do a designated activity such as 10 shoulder touches. The taggers may not tag a pair of students 2 times in a row. The students with the most creatures at the end of the song (or designated time) become the new king and queen.

Variations

Older students can have two different activities to complete before returning to the game, one for a drop and one for a tag. Younger students may have a designated locomotor skill such as sliding or walking to use during the game. Rotate taggers instead of winning the chance to be a tagger.

○ CREATE A DEFINITION

Equipment

- ▶ Markerboard and markers
- ▶ Team warm-up cards (CD, Level 3 Teamwork\Activities\Create a Definition)
- ▶ Small parachute (third grade)
- ▶ 24-inch beach ball (third grade)
- ▶ 2 unused plungers (fourth grade)
- ▶ A basketball resting on a deck ring (fourth grade)
- ▶ A basketball hoop (fourth grade)
- ▶ Plunger duct-taped to an eight-foot PVC pole (fourth grade)
- ▶ 2 ten-foot PVC poles (fourth grade)

Description

This activity gives third- and fourth-grade students a chance to connect, communicate, and collaborate. As students make connections, they see and feel what good teamwork is. They learn the importance of communication and get to practice good communication both by participating in team challenges and through discussion. Students discover that collaborating is the planning process that is essential to positive teamwork.

Start the class with a team warm-up done in their squad groups, using the team warm-up cards found on the CD (Level 3 Teamwork\Activities\Create a Definition). (More on the team warm-up concept is in Glover and Midura 1998.) Once students are done, we meet at the marker board and list what worked well in meeting the warm-up challenges and what did not.

I then divide the class in half. Half of the class participates in a team challenge while the other half watches. The third grade uses a Parachute Challenge, while the fourth grade tries to solve the Plunger Ball Challenge. The half that is not involved first in the challenge watches for positive actions that lead to good teamwork or negative actions that prevent a positive outcome.

level 3

teamwork

Parachute Challenge (third grade): Lay the parachute open on the floor and place the beach ball a few feet away. The challenge is to have the team move the beach ball once around the edge of the parachute while holding the parachute. No team member may touch the beach ball with his hands.

Plunger Ball Challenge (fourth grade): Set up the activity in a basketball key area. Place a basketball resting on a deck ring on the three-point arch at the top of the key. Place two plungers on either side of the basketball. Lay the eight-foot pole with the attached plunger on the floor under the basket. Place the two ten-foot poles on the floor between the basketball and the basket. The team's challenge is to get the basketball into the basket. No player may touch the ball and the ball may not touch the floor. All the equipment must be used at sometime during the challenge. Hands become part of the ten-foot pole if holding the pole. The plunger poles must stay within two to three feet of the basket.

Based on D.W. Midura and D.R. Glover, 2005, *Essentials of team building: Principles and practices* (Champaign, IL: Human Kinetics).

Team Warm-Up

All exercises are done as a team. A leader starts the group and tells them when to move on to the next exercise. You are a team; stay together.

- Do 10 curls at the same time in a circle, giving high fives on the way up.
- Do the #4 stretch slowly on each leg for a slow count of 20, counting together.
- Do 5 push-ups.
- Jump rope 20 times.
- Jog one lap and chant, "I love PE!"

From S. Hagenbach, 2011, *Teaching children responsible behavior: A complete toolkit* (Champaign, IL: Human Kinetics).

Team warm-up card for the Create a Definition activity.

After a few minutes of working on the challenges, the groups come to the marker board, and we discuss what we saw. From this class discussion we start two lists: one for positive actions that lead to good teamwork and another for negative actions that obstruct good teamwork. It is now time to switch roles. The class is made aware that the second group has an advantage in solving the challenge and in demonstrating good teamwork. After a few minutes we again all meet at the marker board and discuss what we saw and add to the list any new observations. With the use of these lists, the class then creates its own definition of teamwork. The lesson is ended with any cooperative tag game.

I post these definitions in the gym and in the hall outside their individual classroom doors. If a class is having difficulty working at Level 3 Teamwork, I can always refer to the definition. I can remind the students that this is their determination about what needs to be done to have great teamwork. They chose the actions. The following definitions are some of my favorites that classes have created through the years:

▶ Teamwork is learning from mistakes and using cooperation to make a plan that helps the team reach a goal: making sure everybody is in it together.

▶ Teamwork is everyone working together to make a plan, sharing jobs, and remembering there is no "I" in TEAM.

▶ Teamwork is working together as friends, doing your job correctly, sharing ideas, and listening so you can reach your goal.

▶ Teamwork is being respectful to each other while making a plan and being responsible to do your best to help achieve the team's goal, making sure everyone is included.

You can see a common thread in these definitions: teamwork involves planning. This is by design. The idea of a team needing a plan is planted early by my questioning and

level 3

teamwork

my verbal observations about how each group is working together. Make this activity your own. If you feel there is an important aspect of teamwork you want your students to discover, plant your own seed.

○ CREATE A GAME

Equipment

▶ Cones

▶ Hoops

▶ Yarn balls

▶ Playground balls

▶ Targets, such as bowling pins or laundry baskets

▶ Poly spots

▶ Beanbags

Description

Once we have created the teamwork definition, I introduce the concept of sportsmanship with the use of the reader, "Teamwork + Sportsmanship = A GREAT game." (The reader is on the CD, Level 3 Teamwork\Reflection\Reader.) I have a set of class copies laminated; we read the short narratives in class and talk about sportsmanship. I also display the Sportsmanship poster (on the CD, Level 3 Teamwork\Posters). Then we play a game. During this unit there are three foci: sportsmanship as students play a variety of games, teamwork as they create games, and the purpose of rules.

The next class we talk about the purpose of rules and what goes into creating a game using the Create a Game worksheet as a guide. The Create a Game worksheet is found on the CD (Level 3 Teamwork\Activities\Create a Game). Rules make games safe, fun, and fair, and tell us how to play. I tell students that when they're creating a game, the following elements need to be considered: the rules, player skills, safety, equipment, game set up, the game type of game, and the name. We then play a game or two and discuss the game played using the Create a Game worksheet as a guide.

Once we have played a variety of games, it is now the students' turn to create their own games.

Students are randomly put on teams, and we review the class definition of teamwork. Each team is given a Create a Game worksheet and allowed to choose from a variety of equipment to create their game. Their first task should be to pick the skills they want to incorporate into the game and determine what type of game they want to create: a cooperative game, a fitness game, a competitive game, or a skill game.

Students have a day or two to create their game, and then they show their game to the class. Uncomplicated games with little set up can be played by the whole class. Games with complicated rules and larger set ups are just demonstrated with helpers.

○ CONFLICT RESOLUTION REVIEW

When the need arises, I review the conflict resolution method of using the levels to solve problems that was taught in second grade. I may do this at various times:

▶ Before a class in which we will be doing an activity where problems tend to arise.

▶ If a public situation arises during class, we may walk through the method together. (I would not use a private situation in front of the whole class)

▶ I may take a week, and at the end of each class, talk through one scenario a day.

level 3

teamwork

Teamwork + Sportsmanship = A Great Game

Teamwork is more than friends helping each other meet challenges and solve problems. It involves having a plan and showing respect. Showing respect not only to your teammates but also to the fans, officials, and other team is part of good *sportsmanship*. Good teamwork and sportsmanship take practice; you need to think about what is right and then try to do it. Your physical education teacher has been giving you the opportunity to practice these skills in class. Have you ever thought about how your choices and actions affect the people in your class? These short stories show how your choice of having good or poor teamwork or sportsmanship can affect others.

Good teamwork involves sharing, caring, compromising, taking turns, being helpful, accepting differences, and planning.

Good sportsmanship involves respect for the rules, officials, coaches, fans, and ALL players while being able to win without bragging and lose without pouting.

The Jaguars were down over 20 points against the Thunder with just over a minute left in the game. The Jaguar coach was ready to substitute some players who had not played much in the game. In basketball, players cannot substitute unless there is a violation, a foul, or a time-out.

The Jaguars were out of time-outs, and seconds were ticking away. The Thunder's coach saw the eager Jaguar players hoping to get into the game and called a time-out for the other team.

Good sportsmanship or good teamwork?
How did this choice affect others?

In physical education Mr. V. is constantly telling us to play our position. He says it will help all of us become better players. Brad always misses the ball in volleyball.

I really wanted to run in front of him and bump the ball over the net. I played my position and reminded Brad how to be ready for the ball. After two misses, Brad hit the ball over! He gave me the biggest smile!

Good sportsmanship or good teamwork?
How did this choice affect others?

At recess we had a great kickball game going. I had made two home runs before the bell rang. Nicole, my friend on the other team, hadn't had a very good game. I could tell she was a little upset. I could have made a great catch to get the last out and asked if she would be on my team again next recess.

Good sportsmanship or good teamwork?
How did this choice affect others?

The neighborhood kids were getting together to play a pickup game of soccer at the park. I usually play goalie and am pretty good at it. The new kid who just moved in last month asked if he could play goalie. I was surprised because I am always goalie. I thought about it and then decided maybe we could compromise. I would play goalie for 10 minutes, and then he could play goalie for 10 minutes. We did Rock-Paper-Scissors to decide who should go first. He won, so I had to play forward. I scored a goal! Hey, I can be good at different positions!

Good sportsmanship or good teamwork?
How did this choice affect others?

From S. Hagenbach, 2011, *Teaching children responsible behavior: A complete toolkit* (Champaign, IL: Human Kinetics).

The reader for Level 3 Teamwork can be used in the Create a Game activity.

Display the sportsmanship poster when initiating the Create a Game activity.

Good sportsmanship is respecting the rules, officials, coaches, fans, and ALL players while knowing how to win without bragging and lose without pouting.

From S. Hagenbach, 2011, *Teaching children responsible behavior: A complete toolkit* (Champaign, IL: Human Kinetics).

Create a Game

Team members' names _____

Name of game _____

Equipment needed _____

Safety hints _____

Skills used in game (include at least two skills) _____

Setup: Draw a picture of the way your game will look at the beginning of the game.

From S. Hagenbach, 2011, *Teaching children responsible behavior: A complete toolkit* (Champaign, IL: Human Kinetics).

Use the Create a Game worksheet to help students create games.

Reflecting on Level 3 Teamwork

Both the thumbs-up assessment and the level touch posters (found on the CD in the All Levels folder) can be used at the end of class to reflect on the students' behavior choices while demonstrating Level 3 Teamwork. As with the other two levels, there is a graphing activity. After reading the story "Who Will You Be in PE?" we review what a Friendly does. As the students name a quality of a Friendly, I put the corresponding graph piece in the pocket chart. The qualities are as follows: A Friendly shares, takes turns, is helpful, is polite, is a friend with everybody, compromises, compliments, and makes people feel good. Over the next few classes, as we do the various Friendly activities, we place a Friendly graph piece next to the quality we practiced. Graph pieces are found on the CD (Level 3 Teamwork\Reflection\Graph).

You can also use the Friendly graph to prepare students for a cooperative activity. Place in the graph the qualities of a Friendly that you want the students to concentrate on while students participate in a cooperative activity. Discuss these qualities before the activity and then make the graph afterward.

The homework and assessment activities for Level 3 Teamwork are similar to those found in the other two levels with an added praise phrase activity you can use with second or third graders. The kindergarten activity has students drawing themselves being a Friendly. Then they add a conversation bubble to the picture. First grade students draw a line from a picture of a Friendly to the pictures on the sheet that show people demonstrating the qualities of a Friendly. This could be used as a formal assessment. Second grade students have a word search, and third graders have a crossword puzzle. The fourth grade homework asks students how they could show teamwork in three different situations: the classroom, the gym, and at home. All homework is found on the CD in Level 3 Teamwork\Reflection\Homework and Assessments.

The reader introduces the concept of sportsmanship and relates it to teamwork. This can be used with a Create a Game unit. It is also a great introduction to an all-school field day or an Olympic Games Day. It is found on the CD in Level 3 Teamwork\Reflection\Reader.

Level touch chart.

From S. Hagenbach, 2011, *Teaching children responsible behavior: A complete toolkit* (Champaign, IL: Human Kinetics).

level 3

teamwork

Level touch target poster.

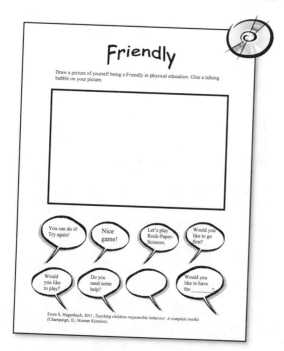

Graph pieces for teamwork reflection activities.

Draw a line to those who are being a Friendly.

Draw a picture of yourself being a Friendly.

Friendly

Find the words in the word search that describe what a Friendly is or does.

helpful	take turns	compromise	share
praise phrase	feel good	teamwork	polite
everyone's friend	rock	paper	scissors
don't brag	congratulate		

H	E	L	P	F	U	L	Z	G	O	P	K	D	F	J
C	V	C	R	W	E	R	Y	U	I	O	P	L	K	P
P	C	O	N	G	R	A	T	U	L	A	T	E	V	R
S	X	M	I	V	S	H	A	R	E	S	B	N	M	A
C	E	P	S	T	Y	U	K	O	O	P	P	P	L	I
I	F	R	E	D	F	E	E	L	G	O	O	D	H	S
S	A	O	P	O	U	N	T	R	F	S	L	Y	W	E
S	O	M	H	N	S	R	U	H	R	T	I	F	F	P
O	D	I	R	T	C	O	R	G	D	G	T	V	G	H
R	F	S	A	B	Q	C	N	W	K	K	E	N	N	R
S	G	E	S	R	A	K	S	D	L	G	A	I	S	A
Y	H	T	E	A	M	W	O	R	K	W	D	U	G	S
U	J	V	S	G	F	Y	R	S	P	A	P	E	R	E
I	K	C	B	N	T	W	D	Y	Y	A	E	H	Y	C
E	V	E	R	Y	O	N	E	S	F	R	I	E	N	D

From S. Hagenbach, 2011, *Teaching children responsible behavior: A complete toolkit* (Champaign, IL: Human Kinetics).

Teamwork Word Search activity.

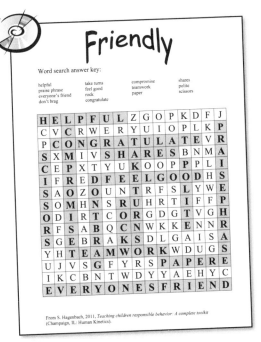

Friendly

Word search answer key:

helpful	take turns	compromise	shares
praise phrase	feel good	teamwork	polite
everyone's friend	rock	paper	scissors
don't brag	congratulate		

H	E	L	P	F	U	L	Z	G	O	P	K	D	F	J
C	V	C	R	W	E	R	Y	U	I	O	P	L	K	P
P	C	O	N	G	R	A	T	U	L	A	T	E	V	R
S	X	M	I	V	S	H	A	R	E	S	B	N	M	A
C	E	P	X	T	Y	U	K	O	O	P	P	P	L	I
I	F	R	E	D	F	E	E	L	G	O	O	D	H	S
S	A	O	Z	O	U	N	T	R	F	S	L	Y	W	E
S	O	M	H	N	S	R	U	H	R	T	I	F	F	P
O	D	I	R	T	C	O	R	G	D	G	T	V	G	H
R	F	S	A	B	Q	C	N	W	K	K	E	N	N	R
S	G	E	B	R	A	K	S	D	L	G	A	I	S	A
Y	H	T	E	A	M	W	O	R	K	W	D	U	G	S
U	J	V	S	G	F	Y	R	S	P	A	P	E	R	E
I	K	C	B	N	T	W	D	Y	Y	A	E	H	Y	C
E	V	E	R	Y	O	N	E	S	F	R	I	E	N	D

From S. Hagenbach, 2011, *Teaching children responsible behavior: A complete toolkit* (Champaign, IL: Human Kinetics).

Key for Teamwork Word Search activity.

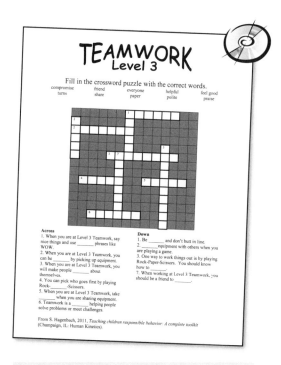

TEAMWORK
Level 3

Fill in the crossword puzzle with the correct words.

compromise	friend	everyone	helpful	feel good
turns	share	paper	polite	praise

Across
1. When you are at Level 3 Teamwork, say nice things and use _____ phrases like WOW.
2. When you are at Level 3 Teamwork, you can be _____ by picking up equipment.
3. When you are at Level 3 Teamwork, you will make people _____ about themselves.
4. You can pick who goes first by playing Rock-_____-Scissors.
5. When you are at Level 3 Teamwork, take _____ when you are sharing equipment.
6. Teamwork is a _____ helping people solve problems or meet challenges.

Down
1. Be _____ and don't butt in line.
2. _____ equipment with others when you are playing a game.
3. One way to work things out is by playing Rock-Paper-Scissors. You should know how to _____.
7. When working at Level 3 Teamwork, you should be a friend to _____.

From S. Hagenbach, 2011, *Teaching children responsible behavior: A complete toolkit* (Champaign, IL: Human Kinetics).

Teamwork Crossword activity.

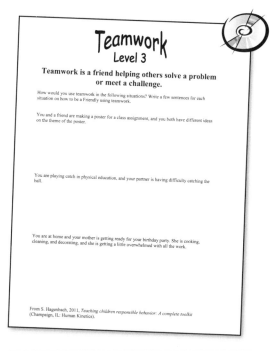

Teamwork
Level 3

Teamwork is a friend helping others solve a problem or meet a challenge.

How would you use teamwork in the following situations? Write a few sentences for each situation on how to be a Friendly using teamwork.

You and a friend are making a poster for a class assignment, and you both have different ideas on the theme of the poster.

You are playing catch in physical education, and your partner is having difficulty catching the ball.

You are at home and your mother is getting ready for your birthday party. She is cooking, cleaning, and decorating, and she is getting a little overwhelmed with all the work.

From S. Hagenbach, 2011, *Teaching children responsible behavior: A complete toolkit* (Champaign, IL: Human Kinetics).

Teamwork All Day activity.

Once all three levels have been introduced and practiced, students may periodically fill out a How Are You Doing assessment found on the CD in the All Levels folder. There is a simple one that students fill in with a smiling face, a straight face, or a frowning face. There is an advanced one that students complete by looking at outcomes specified by the national standards and checking those they have achieved.

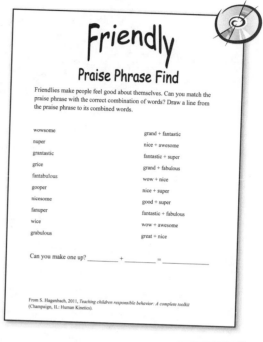

Friendly
Praise Phrase Find

Friendlies make people feel good about themselves. Can you match the praise phrase with the correct combination of words? Draw a line from the praise phrase to its combined words.

wowsome	grand + fantastic
nuper	nice + awesome
grantastic	fantastic + super
grice	grand + fabulous
fantabulous	wow + nice
gooper	nice + super
nicesome	good + super
fanuper	fantastic + fabulous
wice	wow + awesome
grabulous	great + nice

Can you make one up? _____ + _____ = _____

From S. Hagenbach, 2011, *Teaching children responsible behavior: A complete toolkit* (Champaign, IL: Human Kinetics).

Teamwork Praise Phrase activity.

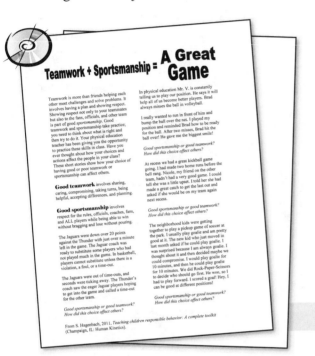

Teamwork + Sportsmanship = A Great Game

Teamwork is more than friends helping each other meet challenges and solve problems. It involves having a plan and showing respect. Showing respect not only to your teammates but also to the fans, officials, and other team is part of good sportsmanship. Good teamwork and sportsmanship take practice; you need to think about what is right and then try to do it. Your physical education teacher has been giving you the opportunity to practice these skills in class. Have you ever thought about how your choices and actions affect the people in your class? These short stories show how your choice of having good or poor teamwork or sportsmanship can affect others.

Good teamwork involves sharing, caring, compromising, taking turns, being helpful, accepting differences, and planning.

Good sportsmanship involves respect for the rules, officials, coaches, fans, and ALL players while being able to win without bragging and lose without pouting.

The Jaguars were down over 20 points against the Thunder with just over a minute left in the game. The Jaguar coach was ready to substitute some players who had not played much in the game. In basketball, players cannot substitute unless there is a violation, a foul, or a time-out.

The Jaguars were out of time-outs, and seconds were ticking away. The Thunder's coach saw the eager Jaguar players hoping to get into the game and called a time-out for the other team.

Good sportsmanship or good teamwork?
How did this choice affect others?

In physical education Mr. V. is constantly telling us to play our position. He says it will help all of us become better players. Brad always misses the ball in volleyball.

I really wanted to run in front of him and bump the ball over the net. I played my position and reminded Brad how to be ready for the ball. After two misses, Brad hit the ball over! He gave me the biggest smile!

Good sportsmanship or good teamwork?
How did this choice affect others?

At recess we had a great kickball game going. I had made two home runs before the bell rang. Nicole, my friend on the other team, hadn't had a very good game. I could tell she was a little upset. I told her she had made a great catch to get the last out and asked if she would be on my team again next recess.

Good sportsmanship or good teamwork?
How did this choice affect others?

The neighborhood kids were getting together to play a pickup game of soccer at the park. I usually play goalie and am pretty good at it. The new kid who just moved in last month asked if he could play goalie. I was surprised because I am always goalie. I thought about it and then decided maybe we could compromise. I would play goalie for 10 minutes, and then he could play goalie for 10 minutes. We did Rock-Paper-Scissors to decide who should go first. He won, so I had to play forward. I scored a goal! Hey, I can be good at different positions!

Good sportsmanship or good teamwork?
How did this choice affect others?

From S. Hagenbach, 2011, *Teaching children responsible behavior: A complete toolkit* (Champaign, IL: Human Kinetics).

Teamwork reader.

How Are You Doing? Level Check

Name _____

Level 1
RESPECT

Level 2
CHALLENGE
I think and practice.

Level 3
TEAMWORK
I am a Friendly.

How Are You Doing? Level Check

Name _____

Level 1
RESPECT

Level 2
CHALLENGE
I think and practice.

Level 3
TEAMWORK
I am a Friendly.

How Are You Doing? Level Check

Name _____

Level 1
RESPECT

Level 2
CHALLENGE
I think and practice.

Level 3
TEAMWORK
I am a Friendly.

How Are You Doing? Level Check

Name _____

Level 1
RESPECT

Level 2
CHALLENGE
I think and practice.

Level 3
TEAMWORK
I am a Friendly.

From S. Hagenbach, 2011, *Teaching children responsible behavior: A complete toolkit* (Champaign, IL: Human Kinetics).

How Are You Doing?

Student _____   Teacher _____

Put a + in the box if the statement is something you do most of the time in physical education.
Put a √ in the box if the statement is something you do sometimes in physical education.
Put a – in the box if the statement is something you could improve on in physical education.

Level 1 Respect	Level 2 Challenge	Level 3 Teamwork
I use honesty to follow rules.	I practice, practice, practice until my teacher signals the end.	I try not to argue and I use acceptable conflict resolution during class.
I use equipment the right way and take care of it.	I work independently and think, think, think while practicing.	I regularly encourage others and I don't use put-downs.
I keep myself and others safe.	I challenge myself without my teacher's reminders.	I cooperate with ALL class members by taking turns and sharing equipment.
I show respect for people and every child by being kind, taking turns, sharing, and not interfering.	I try new skills and movements willingly.	I am a friend to **all**.
I listen attentively to my teacher and follow directions.	I participate even when I'm not successful.	I help others solve problems or meet challenges.
I take responsibility for my own behavior.		

If you marked any box with a √ or –, how can you improve your choices?

What is the level you work at the best? Why?

From S. Hagenbach, 2011, *Teaching children responsible behavior: A complete toolkit* (Champaign, IL: Human Kinetics).

How Are You Doing assessment for grades K-2.

How Are You Doing assessment for grades 3-4.

level 3

teamwork

Communicating With Parents

Part of effective teaching is setting clear expectations for your students. This leads to greater learning and helps create a positive learning environment. Parents should also know your expectations. They will be interested in what their children are learning.

The CD includes two letters you can send to parents for this unit: one explaining the three levels (in the All Levels folder) and another discussing the Friendly story (Level 3 Teamwork\Communication). A pledge sheet for the student to sign may be put on the back of the parent letter. This gives the student the power to choose to be a Friendly. Remember there is power in choice, and with it comes the feeling of satisfaction for doing the right things. Rewards for doing well are not necessary.

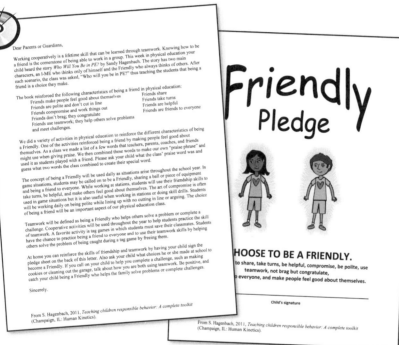

Parent note explaining the Friendly story and student pledge.

Parent note explaining the three levels.

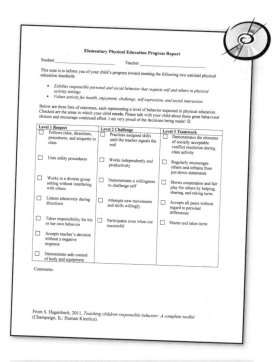

Progress report for students who are doing well.

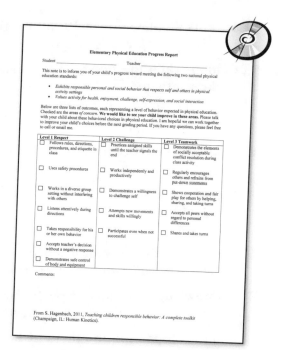

Progress report for students who need improvement.

Another communication tool is the Elementary Physical Education Progress Report based on the NASPE national standards and outcomes. Teachers may use either the *concern* report or the *excelling* report as needed to inform parents of their child's progress between grading periods. This will help avoid surprises to parents at grading periods. Both letters are on the CD in the All Levels folder.

Supporting Standards and Performance Outcomes

All of our activities and lesson designs should support our standards, benchmarks, and outcomes. NASPE National Standard 5: Exhibits responsible personal and social behavior that respects self and others in physical activity settings (NASPE 2004) is met through Level 3 Teamwork. Some performance outcomes (NASPE 2004) are listed here as examples of those that relate to teamwork.

With each sample outcome, I have also included some corresponding child-friendly learning targets written as *I can* statements that refer to teamwork in terms of the standards and outcomes. The push in our district, as it is in education nationally, is to provide students with learning targets, in the belief that students learn more if they know what they are expected to learn. These targets should be written in child-friendly language and should be posted in the classroom. Teachers should address these targets at some time in their lessons. We strive to post our learning targets in every subject: math, reading, physical education, art, music, social studies, and science.

level 3

teamwork

Accepts all playmates without regard to personal difference.
– *I can be a friend to everyone.*

Demonstrates the elements of socially acceptable conflict resolution during class activity.
– *I can use Rock-Paper-Scissors to solve disagreements.*
– *I can solve problems by using the levels.*

Regularly encourages others and refrains from put-down statements.
– *I can use praise phrases with my classmates.*

Invites a peer to take his or her turn at a piece of apparatus before repeating a turn.
– *I can take turns with my classmates.*

Works in a diverse group setting without interfering with others.
– *I can be polite and not interfere with classmates' activities.*

Acknowledges the strong performance of another despite a loss to them.
– *I can congratulate the other team, win or lose.*

Shows compassion to others by helping them.
– *I can be helpful.*
– *I can share.*

Works cooperatively within a diverse group.
– *I can help classmates solve problems or meet challenges.*

Works productively with a partner to improve performance.
– *I can help classmates solve problems or meet challenges.*

Summary

Being a friend and having the skills to work on a team are life skills that will both help your students be successful in life and be happy also. Students working at Level 3 Teamwork will learn to get along within a diverse group through respect, kindness, and empathy. This will help students in the future to achieve healthy personal relationships that are so important in life.

level 3

teamwork

Who Will You Be in PE?

Sandy Hagenbach

I-MEs think only of themselves.

Friendlies think of others —they care!

Would YOU like to have the blue ball?

Friendlies share.

Who will you

be in PE?

I-MEs think only of themselves.

Friendlies think of others —they care!

Who will you

be in PE?

I-MEs think only of themselves.

You stink!
I want to be the best!
Let **ME** be the best!

Friendlies think of others —they care!

Friendlies make people feel good about themselves.

Who will you

be in PE?

I-MEs think only of themselves.

Friendlies think of others —they care!

Friendlies work things out by compromising.

Who will you

be in PE?

I-MEs think only of themselves.

Friendlies think of others —they care!

Who will you

be in PE?

I-MEs think only of themselves.

I want to be in the front. Let **ME** be first in line!

Friendlies think of others —they care!

Friendlies are polite and don't butt in line.

Who will you

be in PE?

I-MEs think only of themselves.

Friendlies think of others —they care!

Who will you

be in PE?

I-MEs think only of themselves.

Friendlies think of others —they care!

You played a great game. Let's play again tomorrow!

Friendlies congratulate instead of bragging.

Who will you

be in PE?

I-MEs think only of themselves.

34

Friendlies think of others —they care!

I'll help you get ready for the big game. Let's play catch!

Friendlies use teamwork, helping others solve problems or meet challenges.

Who will you

be in PE?

I choose to be a Friendly!

A Friendly

- shares
- takes turns
- makes people feel good about themselves
- works things out by compromising
- is a friend to everyone
- is polite and doesn't butt in line
- is helpful
- congratulates instead of bragging
- uses teamwork, helping others solve problems or meet challenges

References

Albert, L. (1996). *Cooperative discipline*. Circle Pines, MN: American Guidance Service.

Bailey, B. (2001). *Conscious discipline: 7 basic skills for brain smart classroom management*. Oviedo, FL: Loving Guidance.

Biehler, R., & Snowman, J. (1997). *Psychology applied to teaching, 8th edition*. Boston: Houghton Mifflin.

Canter, L., & Canter, M. (1976). *Assertive discipline A take charge approach for today's educator*. Santa Monica, CA: Canter & Associates.

Christensen, J., Halper, A., & Strand, P. (2006). *Schools of fish: Welcome back to the reason you became an educator*. Burnseville, MN: ChartHouse International Learning Corporation.

The Cooper Institute, Meredith, M., & Welk, G.J., eds. (2010). *Fitnessgram/Activitygram test administration manual,,* updated 4th ed. Champaign, IL: Human Kinetics.

The Cooper Institute, Meredith, M., & Welk, G.J., eds. (2005). *Fitnessgram/Activitygram test administration manual,* updated 3rd ed. Champaign, IL: Human Kinetics.

Franklin, A. (2007). Respect (Otis Redding, composer). *Queen of soul: The best of Aretha Franklin* (CD). Warner Music.

Gibbs, J. (2001). *Tribes: A new way of learning and being together*. Windsor, California: Center Source.

Grineski, S. 1996. *Cooperative learning in physical education*. Champaign, IL: Human Kinetics.

Hellison, D. (2003). *Teaching responsibility through physical activity*. Champaign, IL: Human Kinetics.

Kelly, L.E., & Melograno, V.J. (2004). *Developing the physical education curriculum*. Champaign, IL: Human Kinetics.

Kronenberg, C. (1997). *Activities for teaching students to live above the line*. Bloomington, MN: Kronenberg Consulting.

Menken, A., & Zippel, D. (2001). A Star Is Born. *Hercules* (CD). Disney.

Midura, D., & Glover, D. (2005). *Essentials of team building principles and practices*. Champaign, IL: Human Kinetics.

Midura, D., & Glover, D. (1998). *Team building through physical challenges*. Champaign, IL: Human Kinetics.

Millang, Steve & Scelsa, Greg. (2000). Freeze. *Vol. 2: We all live together*. Young Heart Music.

Mollin, F., & Rodrigez, C. (2008). Amigos Forever. *Handy Manny* (CD). Walt Disney Records.

National Association for Sport and Physical Education. (2004). *Moving into the future: National standards for physical education*. 2nd ed. Reston, VA: Author.

Unified School District of De Pere Heritage Mission Statement.

About the Author

Sandy Hagenbach, MS, is a teacher at Heritage Elementary School in De Pere, Wisconsin. She has taught grades K-6 since 1978 and was named Wisconsin AHPERD Elementary Teacher of the Year in 2009. She also received the Golden Apple Award for innovative use of literature in physical education and is certified in adapted physical education. As part of the Wisconsin State Standards team, she helped write Wisconsin's learning priorities.

A Kohl education fellowship recipient in 2010, Hagenbach enjoys golf, swimming, and Nordic walking. Raising a son with autism has influenced Sandy's teaching and has given her a unique perspective on teaching responsible behavior.

Photo by Lisa Jansen

You'll find other outstanding
physical education resources at
www.HumanKinetics.com

CD User Instructions

You can use this CD-ROM on either a Windows-based PC or a Macintosh computer.

Windows

- IBM PC compatible with Pentium processor
- Windows 2000/XP/Vista/7
- Adobe Reader 8.0
- Microsoft Office PowerPoint 2003 or higher
- 4x CD-ROM drive

Macintosh

- Power Mac recommended
- System 10.4 or higher
- Adobe Reader
- Microsoft Office PowerPoint 2004 for MAC or higher
- 4x CD-ROM drive

User Instructions

Windows

1. Insert the *Teaching Children Responsible Behavior: A Complete Toolkit* CD-ROM. (Note: The CD-ROM must be present in the drive at all times.)
2. Select the My Computer icon from the desktop.
3. Select the CD-ROM drive.

Macintosh

1. Insert the *Teaching Children Responsible Behavior: A Complete Toolkit* CD-ROM. (Note: The CD-ROM must be present in the drive at all times.)
2. Double-click the CD icon located on the desktop.
3. Open the file you wish to view. See the 00Start file for a list of the contents.

For customer support, contact Technical Support:

Phone: 217-351-5076 Monday through Friday (excluding holidays) between 7:00 a.m. and 7:00 p.m. (CST).

Fax: 217-351-2674

E-mail: support@hkusa.com